Endorsements

Doug and I began our walk together as young men, as our fathers' sons, and now we have sons of our own. As our culture wastes, lacking direction and conviction, we need the next generation of sons to stand on the truth of God's Word. Within these pages you will find a man whose heart is to see each person he contacts walk with the Lord in everyday circumstances. With wit, humor, and sincerity Doug seeks to capture the picture God has for His children. I am privileged to have called this man my friend for the last 18 years and am blessed to call him my brother in Christ. All those who enter, with a willing heart, will be honed "As iron sharpens iron."

—Dr. Jeremy A. Rogers
Lead Pastor
Arlington Park Baptist Church
Arlington, Texas

It is my privilege to recommend this wonderful book to all who are seeking God's heartbeat for the husband and father in the home. Doug Chumley along with his wife Marcy has set an example of a God-fearing home for their four children. Doug has a desire that all men come to Christ and lead their families into the biblical truths of God's word. He understands that in a day when the father commonly is missing from the home that there needs to be a call back to the correct understanding of fathers throughout our culture. When the truth has been exchanged for a lie and the Gospel of Jesus Christ is taught as religion and not absolute truth, Doug is heralding Christ in the home louder than anyone I know. Doug is a man of great character, and he leads his home with humility and grace. Doug is a caring husband to his wife Marcy, a great father to his beautiful daughter and a true example of a God-fearing man to his three boys. It has been my joy to pastor this family and to watch them grow in the truth of scripture and to see them lead out in ministry here at Pine Island Baptist.

—Tom Dobbs
Senior Pastor
Pine Island Baptist Church
Hempstead, Texas

This is a cutting-edge view of foundational truths that will appeal to men of all generations. In the shifting times we are living in, it is nice to see some solid footing for men to run to on a daily basis to ensure a firm foundation for life. Doug has a unique perspective and a great way of giving relevance to time-tested Scripture. I highly recommend this book to men of all ages.

—Jim Bracelin
Director of Outreach
Silent Word Ministries
Trenton, Georgia

FENCE POSTS

Doug Chumley

LUCIDBOOKS

Fence Posts
Copyright © 2016 by Doug Chumley

Published by Lucid Books in Houston, TX.
www.LucidBooks.net

All rights reserved. No part of this publication may be reproduced, stored in a retrieval system, or transmitted in any form by any means, electronic, mechanical, photocopy, recording, or otherwise, without the prior permission of the publisher, except as provided for by USA copyright law.

Scripture quotations noted as "ESV" are from the ESV® Bible (The Holy Bible, English Standard Version®), copyright © 2001 by Crossway, a publishing ministry of Good News Publishers. Used by permission. All rights reserved.

Scripture quotations noted as "NASB" are taken from the New American Standard Bible®, Copyright © 1960, 1962, 1963, 1968, 1971, 1972, 1973, 1975, 1977, 1995 by The Lockman Foundation. Used by permission. (www.Lockman.org)

Scripture quotations noted as "NKJV" taken from the New King James Version®. Copyright © 1982 by Thomas Nelson. Used by permission. All rights reserved.

First Printing 2016

ISBN 10: 1-63296-080-X
ISBN 13: 978-1-63296-080-1
eISBN 10: 1-63296-081-8
eISBN 13: 978-1-63296-081-8

Special Sales: Most Lucid Books titles are available in special quantity discounts. Custom imprinting or excerpting can also be done to fit special needs. Contact Lucid Books at info@lucidbooks.net.

Contents

Introduction 1

Chapter 1: Why What We Do Matters 5

Chapter 2: Do what's Right, the Right Way, for the Right Reasons because they're Watching 36

Chapter 3: Love Your Wife 50

Chapter 4: Get it Done, Have Fun, and Let them Help 66

Chapter 5: Name 70

Chapter 6: Fighting Evil 73

Endnotes 99

Introduction

I DO NOT WRITE as one who is qualified in and of himself to teach about these things. I write to you as a servant of the Lord to remind you of—and maybe even to introduce some of you to—his call to men.

This world desperately needs, but ruthlessly persecutes, real men. We are falsely accused, penalized, and told to be quiet. We are threatened, and our families are threatened. For a world that revolts against God, we must necessarily be removed because we represent a boundary between right and wrong. We are the bulwark that the Lord has established to stand against evil. But God in his wisdom created us to thrive when our backs are against the wall. That's why I like to watch *Rio Bravo* so much. (If you don't know what I'm talking about, watch it. Love it. Live it.) We who have been established by the Lord are and will always be sustained by his hand as we run this race.

The baton has been handed off to us. Enoch ran with it. Noah, Abraham, Moses, Joshua, Caleb, Elijah, Elisha, and Daniel (you get the idea) all ran with it, looking forward to the day of the Lord. I believe with all of my heart that we are the anchor leg.

In order to preserve the truth for all time, the Lord warns us six different times in the Bible not to move the boundary that has been set up (Deut. 19:14; 27:17; Job 24:2; Prov. 22:28; 23:10;

Hosea 5:10). Two of the six warnings contain references to the boundary having been set up by the ancestors or fathers. God intends for us to be honest and not to encroach upon or steal property that is not ours. He also intended for this principle to apply in other areas of life as evidenced by Hosea's claim that "the princes of Judah have become like those who move a boundary" (5:10 NASB). God has set up boundaries for us to live by. These boundaries are for our good, but over time we have grown resentful and have moved the boundaries, as Psalm 2:2–3 says, "The kings of the earth take their stand, and the rulers take counsel together against the Lord and against His Anointed: 'Let us tear their fetters apart, and cast away their cords from us'" (NASB).

All of this means that men who know, love, and serve the Lord are intended to be part of this boundary. You could say that we are the fence posts that make up the boundary. Think about that. A man ought to be like a fence post. It stands where the builder establishes it, set deep beneath the surface. Some fence posts are steel, iron, aluminum, or wooden, but all are treated to be able to weather well and withstand whatever may try to bend or break them. A fence post stands to be a clear landmark, holding up all the lines or planks attached to it. A fence post may stand doing its job in a remote, neglected corner of the property for decades without notice but will still do what it was created to do just the same. A fence post is always there, without taking a day off.

In the same way, a man established by the Lord will stand, no matter what the circumstances. Some of us are young, old, or somewhere in between; married, single, fathers, or not. Some of us are in environments that are more hostile than others toward God and the people who bear his name. Wherever we may be, the Lord causes his men to stand.

In Genesis 17:1 God said to Abram, "I am God Almighty;

walk before me, and be blameless" (NASB). Now, the name that God calls himself here is "El Shaddai," which in Hebrew means burly and powerful. God reminded Abram that he is the Almighty. Then he told him "walk before Me and be blameless" (17:1 NASB). To walk before the Lord is to walk where he can see us. Almighty God, whose Word and authority are final, said to Abram and says to us "walk before Me and be blameless." We have to walk in the way he has directed us, in the safety of his eyes. When we walk that way, we cannot help but stand because we are sustained by God himself.

Can your family and the people in your life count on you to stand? Do you depend on yourself or do you trust El Shaddai to make you stand?

We have allowed the voices of the world (the whiney voices, I might add) to shame men who live as the God-ordained fence posts for our culture, indoctrinating our children against us. Our culture has gone so far that Paula Cole had to ask the question that we were all thinking: "Where have all the cowboys gone?" Well, mamas, it's time to let your babies grow up to be cowboys.

We have found ourselves in a world where a lawless government robs from its people, hates truth, perverts justice, oppresses its military heroes, despises God, and seeks to silence his people. These criminals carry out their plans because they believe that there are not enough real men left to stop them. Real men have been branded "backward" and "ignorant," and their own children are taught that their parents are wrong. Deconstructionist thinking (which, ironically, is easily deconstructed) has been taught long enough that a significant segment of the population believes that truth, right and wrong, and anything absolute exist only as social constructs.

Our children need real men to stand in their lives—real men who walk blamelessly in the sight of El Shaddai, borne up by nothing more and nothing less than his own hand, as a testimony that is not easily silenced, forgotten, or explained away. Even if those who want us out of the way go so far as to kill us, Psalm 112:6–7 says, "He will never be shaken; the righteous will be remembered forever. He will not fear evil tidings; his heart is steadfast, trusting in the Lord" (NASB).

CHAPTER 1

Why What We Do Matters

OUR ENEMY, THE devil, has a vested interest in destroying your family, so you must have a vested interest in strengthening your family. We cannot underestimate the importance of the family because our enemy will not. If we pay attention, we will quickly understand that the family and each of its members are under assault from every side. Much of the media in popular U. S. culture glamorizes and praises promiscuity and adultery while ignoring or even criticizing faithfulness and marriage. Many prominent filmmakers and songwriters would have us believe that in order to be truly happy and fulfilled with someone, we must first "find ourselves" and see what else is "out there."[1]

Not only does media in our culture rage against God's purpose for the family, but our own social and political climates are hostile as well. Our tax code rewards us for having children, but penalizes us for being married. Men are ridiculed for being faithful husbands and fathers while the unfaithful man is idolized.

You have probably heard many statistics that show that children raised in single-parent homes tend to have dramatically higher rates of many different types of problems, including trouble with the law and poverty. So why would our culture push so hard against the intended structure of the family? The stated reasons for these attacks are numerous, but they all boil down to one reason: our rebellious human nature revolts at the knowledge that we must ultimately give account to someone else.

To acknowledge God is also to acknowledge that we are not him. Since the beginning of time, mankind has followed the lead of our enemy, Satan, and worked hard to undermine everything that is true and that the Lord has said is good. Our enemy knows that if the family, as established by God, can be pushed to the brink of extinction, any semblance of morality and resistance to his agenda will be weak at best.

We can look at the world we live in and realize that it is no longer conducive to the building of strong families. Think about how much time a family gets to spend together in the average week. Mornings are usually a blur of people trying to get to work and school on time. Very few mothers get to stay at home with their young children anymore. The average cost of living is such that very few men earn enough to sustain their households on their own. Those who do it anyway usually do so by a conscious effort to live on a very tight budget. We find even young children in the hands of people other than their parents for most of their waking hours. Evening schedules are usually dictated by extracurricular activities and maybe even late working hours for parents. Add to the mix the ever-increasing expectation that we must tether ourselves to our phones and computers so that we can respond to e-mails and take calls. Then it's no surprise when our children follow our examples by spending an obscene amount of time on phones and stuffing their ears with who knows what. Many parents leave work and, instead of going home, go to a gym for an hour or more.

I am not suggesting that we neglect our work or our health; however, we must not sacrifice our families for our own personal gains. That is the opposite of what family is all about.

We must lead by example and make sure that we are spending time nurturing, playing with, and talking with our families, even if it means laying our own lives down to do so. You heard right. Laying my life down means more than dying for them; it also means putting my life aside for them as directed and exemplified by God. I am sad to say that we live in a culture that does not understand that kind of love.

Many of my peers are perfectly willing to "abort" their own children in the name of convenience or to destroy their own families to pursue their dreams. Then, our most "brilliant" minds engage in studies to try to determine why children and adults are experiencing emotional disorders, depression, and suicidal tendencies at unthinkable rates. We wonder why our children grow up and don't know how to keep their word, how to treat people, how to consider someone outside of themselves, or how to get a job done.

If we as fathers are too busy to spend time with our families, then we're too busy. Our career goals are not as important as the lives of our family members. Do not imagine that your wife and kids need a bigger house and more stuff more than they need a real man in their lives. Our wives need to see our vows fulfilled to them every day without exception. Our kids need to know that we are proud to be their daddies. Our every word and action should be a testament to them of the ferocity and the unbreakable tenderness of our love for them. From comforting them to disciplining them and everything in between, the love of their one and only daddy needs to be an ever-present anchor for them.

In a world that people have shaped to be destructive to the family, we have to rise and be the heroes that we always wanted to be. God has called you and me to be the fence posts, the immovable men who will look the whole world in the face and say, "I will love my family and lay my life down for them."

Joshua: The Upbringing of a Real Man

Joshua's life exemplifies how men are intended to bring other men up to know and trust the Lord. Moses, although not Joshua's father, provided Joshua with guidance, opportunities to learn to lead, and encouragement.

The Training

In Exodus 17, the Amalekite army confronted the Israelites. In verse nine, Moses said to Joshua, "Choose men for us, and go out, fight against Amalek. Tomorrow I will station myself on the top of the hill with the staff of God in my hand" (NASB). Moses entrusted Joshua with the task of choosing the men for the battle and leading them out. Don't miss the rest of the story. Moses helped by holding up the staff during the battle. While Moses held it up, the Israelites prevailed, but when his arms became tired and the staff lowered, the Amalekites pushed Israel's troops back. Then, Aaron and Hur seated Moses on a rock and held his arms up so that the Israelites won the battle. This is a story about men helping men—who are helping men.

Now don't misunderstand the staff. There was nothing magical about the staff. In various places, God chose to manifest his power through the staff; however, we must always read the Bible as a whole, and in doing so we understand that the Holy Spirit lives in us and manifests his power through those who trust the Lord and live according to the Spirit. So for our purposes, we can equate the raising of the staff to our prayers. We are to pray for each other as we strive together to walk in good works, which God prepared for us beforehand (Eph. 2:10).

This battle is a beautiful picture of how God's men are supposed to bring the next generation along. Moses sent Joshua not only to choose the men who would go and fight, but also to lead them into the battle. On a *much* smaller scale, this episode reminds me of a time when I was in high school and my daddy gave me the keys to his pickup to go on a date. (Like I said, *much* smaller.) This vote of confidence showed that Moses trusted Joshua's relationship with the Lord. And Moses let Joshua know that he would be interceding for him all the while. Both men trusted each other as they both entrusted themselves to God.

The Decision

Exodus 32 finds the children of Israel growing impatient with God and making an idol, the infamous golden calf. This horrific rebellion occurred in Moses' absence. Significantly, Joshua was also missing. Verse 17 says that Joshua heard the sound of the people and mistook the noise for fighting. Based on Joshua's character, as revealed through his actions throughout his life, it's safe to go out on a limb and say that had he been there when the rebellion began, he would either have been killed for standing in the way or there would have been no rebellion. Joshua was fit to lead the people into the land when the time came because he trusted God and tried to persuade the Israelites to do the same; however, he was also able to lead the people after Moses because he had kept his way pure during this dark moment in Israel's history.

Men of all ages, as it was for Joshua, it is imperative that each of us keeps his way pure. Psalm 119:9 famously asks, "How can a young man keep his way pure?" David answers: "By keeping it according to Thy word" (NASB). We have all sinned, but by

God's grace, we are offered forgiveness. Because of that grace, for the sake of our calling to be God's people in this world, and for the sake of our children, we must always be found standing faithful, having not defiled our garments or compromised the Word of God in our lives. Besides that, life is a lot easier when you don't have skeletons in your closet. Keeping our way pure must start now. If we are not willing to start now, what makes us think that we will be willing later? Joshua understood that he had to stand on the Word of the Lord today.

The Stand

It is also important to point out that Joshua was a leader in his tribe. A reading of Numbers 13:3–15 shows that all the spies were leaders of their tribes. Now it is no surprise that Joshua was considered a respected and trusted head of his tribe; however, Joshua and Caleb stood in the minority when the other revered heads of the tribes of Israel chose to deviate from the Word of the Lord. Like Joshua, we must stand in our families as steady fence posts who will not be moved by popular opinion.

In Numbers 14:9, Joshua and Caleb urged the Israelites saying, "Only do not rebel against the Lord, nor fear the people of the land, for they are our bread; their protection has departed from them, and the Lord is with us. Do not fear them" (NKJV). Joshua and Caleb understood that God was with them and that the protection of the Canaanites was gone.

In verse 10, the people responded by calling for the stoning of Joshua and Caleb. We should expect to be treated as Joshua and Caleb were. The mind that is controlled by the flesh (like ours before we trusted the Lord) is hostile to God and does not want to hear the truth, but Joshua and Caleb knew, as we must know, that nothing excuses us from obeying God. They would rather defy their whole society than to disobey the Lord. The world desperately needs men like these again.

Too many men in our culture are scared to death to be the only one. Joshua and Caleb were not. Since they were not afraid to be the only ones, the Lord said that they would be the only ones from their generation to go into the land that God was giving to the Israelites.

In Numbers 32:12 the Lord said that Caleb and Joshua "wholly followed the Lord" (ESV). For that reason, they were allowed to go where the rest of their generation was disqualified from going. I don't know about you, but I am in awe of imagining God himself saying that. In all honesty, how many of us think and have heard others say, "I hope God can say that about me?" Why don't we stop hoping for that and start living it? Joshua and Caleb didn't stand around hoping that they would do the right thing. They had their hearts set on the Lord, and when God spoke, they built their worlds around it. I don't mean to oversimplify things, but that is what it boils down to. In his strength and by his Holy Spirit, we are called to live as these men did.

The Fulfillment

Forty years went by, and Joshua and Caleb saw every single Israelite who had been twenty or older at the time of the rebellion pass away. But before Moses died, God told him in Deuteronomy 1:38-39 to encourage Joshua because he would be the one to lead the Israelites into the land that God had promised them. Verse 39 says, "Moreover, your little ones who you said would become a prey, and your sons, who this day have no knowledge of good or evil, shall enter there, and I will give it to them, and they shall possess it" (NASB). Just imagine being Joshua in the years right after God had pronounced judgment on the unbelieving Israelites. I imagine him walking through the camp, seeing toddlers playing, and not just speculating, but *knowing* that they would be the army who would one day follow him across the river to take Jericho and everything that lay beyond. God used the very children that the unbelieving thought would fall prey to the Canaanites to be the ones who would go in and defeat the enemy.

Even though it took forty years, Joshua relied on the Lord for his vindication in keeping with the example set by his mentor, Moses. We know from the Bible that Joshua had been Moses' right-hand man from his youth. So encouragement from Moses at such a momentous time in Joshua's life would have carried enormous weight.

In Deuteronomy 3:21–22, we see Moses following through with God's command and encouraging Joshua with these words: "And I commanded Joshua at that time, saying, 'Your eyes have seen all that the Lord your God has done to these two kings [Og and Sihon]; so the Lord shall do to all the kingdoms into which you are about to cross. Do not fear them, for the Lord your God is the one fighting for you'" (NKJV).

In the same way, the Lord intends us to encourage each other to live out the good works that he has prepared for us. Hebrews 10:24–25 reads, "And let us consider how to stimulate one another to love and good deeds, not forsaking our own assembling together, as is the habit of some, but encouraging one another; and all the more, as you see the day drawing near" (NASB). We may have a "Joshua" in our lives. What if Moses had failed to encourage Joshua toward the work that God had prepared for him?

Pick up a copy of *Rocky Balboa*, the sixth installment of the fabled *Rocky* film series for an excellent example of what it looks like to build up the next generation. If you are not familiar with—nay, well versed in—the prior five installments then you will want to procure those as well. Gather your loved ones, and pop some popcorn. Season the popcorn to taste with Creole seasoning (do it!). When the time comes, pay attention to Rocky's speech to his son when he has lost perspective and needs a little redirection from his father. The monologue will give you insight into how one man, in love and in truth, rebukes another. We should never think that we don't need each other or that someone else does not need what the Lord has given us to do or say.

At your leisure, you should also check out *Rocky IV* wherein Sly delivers once again, this time packaging and delivering a scathing commentary on the inherent evils of communism, performance-enhancing drugs, and husbands and wives having the same hair styles.

All these building blocks that we have examined combined to construct a man who was an absolutely vital leader of God's people (Joshua, not Rocky). Judges 2:7 says, "And the people served the Lord all the days of Joshua, and all the days of the elders who survived Joshua, who had seen all the great work of the Lord which he had done for Israel" (NASB). Joshua and the elders who served under his leadership led Israel to follow the Lord. When the other leaders of the nation of Israel moved the boundary, Joshua stood as the fence post that God had established.

In the same way, we must be established by God and build our lives around his Word. Men, what we do matters. Will we be "Moseses" and bring up a generation to trust the Lord? Will we be "Joshuas" and listen to and learn from the fence posts in our lives? Will we still stand when an entire nation turns its back on the Lord? Joshua's best-known words underscore the importance of this resolve:

> "And if it is disagreeable in your sight to serve the Lord, choose for yourselves today whom you will serve: whether the gods which your fathers served which were beyond

the river, or the gods of the Amorites in whose land you are living; but as for me and my house, we will serve the Lord" (Josh. 24:15 NASB).

The Rechabites

One criminally overlooked spot of the Bible is Jeremiah 35. Jeremiah is, for the most part, a bleak book; but chapter 35 reminds us that in the midst of God's wrath against sin, the Lord blesses those who trust him. If you're not familiar with it, go ahead and read Jeremiah 35 right now. If you are familiar with it, go ahead and read Jeremiah 35 right now. It's good for you. God devoted this chapter of the Bible to recognizing and blessing the obedience of the Rechabites before the whole world for all time. Why? God underscored their behavior because they had obeyed the command that the Lord had given their forefather Jonadab somewhere in the neighborhood of 300 years prior!

The command was, "you shall not drink wine, you or your sons, forever. And you shall not build a house, and you shall not sow seed, and you shall not plant a vineyard, or own one; but in tents you shall dwell all your days, that you may live many days in the land where you sojourn" (Jer. 35:6–7 NASB). The majority of our culture would look at those commands (especially after 300 years) and question their relevance.

"Relevance" is a hot buzzword in many modern American churches, and its danger cannot be stressed enough. Many congregations and ministers tout the relevance of their teaching. The inherent implication is that some teachings in the Bible are irrelevant. That implication may not be intended, but it is nonetheless horrifically arrogant, especially in a world that is already rushing headlong into death because of the belief that man knows better than God. We absolutely must stop centering our churches on "me" and instead, center "me" on the Lord Jesus. How dare I tell the Almighty Creator and Sustainer that I have judged that I don't need to concern myself with thoughts of his, thoughts that he has humbled himself into our filth to deliver to us in the hope of saving our lives?

The descendants of Rechab understood and lived by that principle. And say what you want about them, but they understood that when a father teaches the Word of God to his children, they do well to listen and obey. In Exodus 20:12, the Lord commands us to "Honor your father and your mother, that your days may be prolonged in the land which the Lord your God gives you" (NASB). The Lord says, in Jeremiah 35:16, "Indeed, the sons of Jonadab the son of Rechab have observed the command of their father which he commanded them, which he commanded them, but this people [the men of Judah and the inhabitants of Jerusalem (v.13)] has not listened to Me" (NASB), making a clear distinction between the life of obedience and the life of self-indulgence.

God sets the Rechabites up as an example of how we are to hear, trust, and obey. Like the Rechabites, we have to look at the teachings of the forefathers in our lives who have honored the Lord. We also have to teach our children to obey the Lord without exception. The Rechabites were real men. They didn't care what anyone else was doing or what anyone else had. They knew the command of the Lord and they held to it.

We are living in one of our nation's darkest times in its history right now. We have found ourselves here in large part due to our refusal to listen to the wisdom of those who have gone before us who know and honor God. Many Americans have neglected the teaching of those who asked the blessing and direction of the Lord to form the greatest nation the world has ever known. We have dismissed the warnings from God's own Word that were heeded by those who went before us and sacrificed their lives to protect us from days like these.

In this world, we are the fence posts that the Lord has driven into the ground and established to stand, like the Rechabites, as an example of how a real man builds his house on the Rock. And, when the storm rages it will surely stand.

Jeremiah 35 ends with a blessing from God given to the Rechabites. "Jonadab the son of Rechab shall not lack a man to stand before Me always" (Jer. 35:19 NASB). What the Rechabites did mattered to their descendants. Each of us wants to know that his family is and always will be safe and that they will love the Lord. Pray for your family. Stop thinking about it, and start living in obedience to the Word of God.

If anything ever stands in the way, confess it to the Lord who has always loved you. Tell him about it and ask him to help. He has already proven no length is too far for him to go when his children run to him.

Joseph

We tend to look at Mary and think about how humble, obedient, and faithful to the Lord she must have been for God to choose her as Jesus' mother. We are right to think those things, but Joseph often goes overlooked. The cool thing is that he doesn't seem like the kind of guy who would mind being overlooked. That very quality is what we should pay attention to. Because Joseph was a man who built his life around the Lord, God was able to use him to raise and even protect his Son's life.

Matthew 1:18–25 tells the story of a great man. It became known that Mary, Joseph's promised wife, was pregnant. Verse 19 says that Joseph "being a just man" still wanted to save her from the consequences of adultery, which would have been death, so he determined to release her from her commitment to him secretly. Joseph was not interested in his own vindication or in his own pride. Instead, he concerned himself with doing what was right (this is reason #1 that he was able to be used by God).

In verses 20–23, an angel appeared to Joseph in a dream and told him what the Lord was doing and what Joseph should do. Then, in verses 24–25, Joseph showed us what a real man does when God speaks. Joseph awoke from the dream and immediately changed his life's direction to suit the Word of the Lord. Not only did Joseph take Mary as his wife, but he "did not know her till she had brought forth her firstborn Son" (Matt. 1:25 NKJV).

He also gave him the name that God had spoken to him. Joseph was not a man who was concerned about his rights or getting what was his (reason #2 that he was able to be used by God).

Later, Joseph even saved Jesus' life when Herod had countless baby boys from among his subjects murdered because he wanted Jesus dead. An angel appeared to Joseph again in a dream in Matthew 2:13 and told him to do something absurd. He told Joseph to move himself and his family out of the country until he would tell him to bring them back. Once again, Joseph changed his life to honor the Word of the Lord. As a result, Jesus survived.

The world needs us to follow in the footsteps of Joseph. When the Lord speaks (and he has spoken plenty), it should alter our lives. God has not suggested that we consider being honest. He has not recommended that we think about tithing and attending church. He does not think that it might be a good idea if we would love him and love people. So we need not act like the Word of the Lord is an obsolete book of fables and irrelevant rules. The Word of the one God is the means by which he created the universe from absolutely nothing. The Word of the Lord is Jesus himself. The Almighty God's Word is the sword that will strike the nations. And as Joseph did, we should view God's Word as such.

In your home, is the Word of the Lord honored and obeyed, or is it more of a superstition that is given enough attention to keep it appeased? Do your children know that their daddy has forsaken whatever parts of his life don't work with God's Word? Does your wife know that her husband, who she has gone all in with, has built their home on the Rock? If the answers are not what they should be, then talk with the Lord. Let him show you how it's done. What Joseph did matters to all of us. God was able to call Joseph to raise Jesus and to make the home that he would grow up in because Joseph honored the Word of the Lord.

Noah: Do We Believe God?

Noah was a man who believed God. In a world where everything true and good was despised, Noah found grace in the eyes of the Lord. In our culture where goodness and truth are increasingly despised, we can and must find grace in the eyes of the Lord so that we and our families will be saved. And we will do it the same way Noah did, by believing God.

Heritage

We can begin by looking at Noah's family—not his wife and sons, but his ancestors. Noah was the son of Lamech, son of Methuselah, son of Enoch. Now, not much is said about Enoch, but what is said is very important. Genesis 5:22–24 tells us that Enoch walked with God and that "he was not, for God took him" (NASB). Hebrews 11:5 tells us that "By faith Enoch was taken up so that he would not see death . . . for he obtained the witness that before his being taken up he was pleasing to God" (NASB). Two verses later, the writer of Hebrews mentions

Enoch's great-grandson, Noah. We often think of Noah as a man alone in an utterly depraved world, and we would be correct; however, Noah's faith was no accident.

We have tremendous influence over our children, and by extension, over their children and so on. It is no coincidence that the man who found grace in the eyes of the Lord was the great-grandson of the man who the Bible notes as having pleased God. We can also tell that Lamech saw the Lord as important because he named his son "Noah," meaning "rest" (Gen. 5:29). When he named Noah, Lamech said, "This one will comfort us concerning our work and the toil of our hands, because of the ground which the Lord has cursed" (5:29 NKJV). Like Enoch and Noah, Lamech was a man who walked with God—a pattern in this family.

Notice that this family raised a Noah in a time when the world was hurtling toward chaos (Gen. 6:1–8). Verse five says, "Then the Lord saw that the wickedness of man was great on the earth, and that every intent of the thoughts of his heart was only evil continually" (NASB). There are three absolutes in that sentence: "every," "only," and "continually." This claim about the people is definite. In those days and the days leading up to them (the earth was a little less than 2,000 years old at the time), Noah's family served God. And in those last days before the flood, Noah, his wife, his boys, and their wives remained faithful. And from the darkness, verse eight says, "But Noah found grace in the eyes of the Lord" (NKJV).[2]

It is painfully apparent that we have many men who have sold out their allegiance to God and his Word for the sake of career goals, financial security, and a variety of alternative pursuits. Younger brothers, many of you know very well that the prevailing current around you is to sell out what you know to be right and wrong for the sake of appearances—appearances in the eyes of girls (usually the wrong ones), "friends," and classmates who will not tolerate anyone who does not play by their social rules. Throughout history, real men, like Noah, have stepped up when called upon. In the words of Mordecai, "who knows whether or not" we have been placed here "for such a time as this" (Esther 4:14 NKJV).

In My House

In my classroom, my students always tell me, "It's nothing we haven't heard before," when they get into trouble for having a filthy mouth. My response never varies: "You haven't heard it from me." They also say, "We're just going to listen to it anyway after your class," when they want to listen to their music in their earphones while working in my class. Again, my invariable response is, "Not in my room." The intent is not meanness, but instead, to teach them that principles are important. Right and wrong are neither relative nor subjective.

Noah was a "just man, perfect in his generations" (Gen. 6:9 NKJV). Noah, like Daniel and his friends, was not a man who accepted defeat at the hands of the flesh. Too many of us sometimes allow sin into our lives as long as it's not "too bad." We tend to shrug it off and console ourselves by saying that it's just the world we live in. That world was not welcome in Noah's house, and we should not welcome it in ours. That world is not welcome where our kids play. It is not welcome in our hearts, minds, and mouths.

God used the same Hebrew word from Genesis 6:9 meaning "complete, perfect or having integrity" when he told Abram to walk before him and be "blameless" in Genesis 17:1. He told Abram to be complete, perfect, and to have integrity because he had chosen Abram to be the founding father of the Hebrew nation, through whom God would reveal himself to the world and bring forth his Son.

Essentially, we are called by God to be complete, perfect, and to have integrity for the same reasons. He wants to use us to reveal himself to the world and to make his Son known. God's calling of his men to righteousness is more than an admirable but lofty goal. It is an imperative if we are serious about being like Noah and saving our families and as many others as possible from the wrath of God's judgment.

You and All Your Household

Genesis 6:22–7:1 is a very soothing passage: "Thus Noah did; according to all that God had commanded him, so he did. Then the Lord said to Noah, 'Come into the ark, you and all your household; because I have seen that you are righteous before Me in this generation'" (NKJV). It wasn't up to Noah to figure anything out. He simply obeyed the Lord.

About 100 years passed between God telling Noah to build the ark and the coming of the flood, during which time Noah just believed God and carried out his Word. And because he did, the Lord told him to "come into the ark, you and all your household" (Gen. 7:1 NKJV). The Lord wants us and our households to be saved as well. And, we will get there the same way Noah did: by believing the Lord. "By faith Noah . . . prepared an ark for the saving of his household" (Heb. 11:7 NKJV). God has also commanded us to prepare for the salvation of our households, and he has told us how. The question is whether we believe him.

Like Noah's family, the Lord wants our families to be saved as well. We can look at the actions of Noah's wife, sons, and daughters-in-law and see that Noah was the kind of man who could tell his family something as (let's be honest) absurd as what he told them, and they believed him for at least 100 years and were saved.

The Almighty God and You

Now we have to stop right here and ask ourselves some serious questions that we likely already know the answers to. If we had been in Noah's place, would our wives, children, and in-laws believe us? Would God even bother to tell us? If the answer to either of those questions is no, then how can we change it? How can we alter the courses of our families?

We must always begin with acknowledgement and repentance. The good news is that the Lord has already given us instructions and examples to follow to get there. Many of us are already even familiar with those instructions and examples, but they won't do us any good unless we allow ourselves to be changed by them. James 1 tells us that we have to read God's Word as though we were looking into a mirror. We look into a mirror to correct our appearances. The mirror does us no good if we walk away forgetting what we have seen.

If we have not been leading our families like we should have been, then we have to repent, and we have to do it now. They may not understand at first, but there is no other way. Self-help books won't save your family. Sending the kids to church won't save your family. Oprah, Dr. Phil, and other highly esteemed advice-givers the world has to offer won't save your family. The Lord alone can save our families. The one God, who took the care to create man by hand when he spoke everything else into existence, can save our families. Don't settle for counterfeits. Don't make your family settle for counterfeits.

Once we have repented and sought the Lord and his Word, what remains is to get up and walk in his ways. I can see Rocky Balboa having just been knocked onto the mat, his vision spinning, searching every corner of his soul for the strength to get back up. Just then, the voice of Mick cuts through the chaos and says "Get up!" God says the same thing to you and me. Don't imagine that Noah never made a mistake. Noah just repented, got up, and fought.

Today

We need to understand that a time comes when it is too late to enter the ark, so to speak. Throughout the Bible and throughout history since the completion of the Bible, God has been and is still very patient with us so that more people will be saved. But in Genesis 7:16, the Lord closed the door of the ark. Those of us with kids know that time is fleeting. We don't have time to "muck about," as the late great Steve Irwin would say if he were here, and take our time to get our acts together. Our kids need us now. Our families need real men now.

As a high school teacher, I can look around daily and see young men whose so-called principles do not match up with their actions. When confronted about it, some of them say that they will do the right things when they are older, but that right now teenagers are supposed to do the things that they are doing. You know, things like constantly pumping their minds full of "musicians" who hate truth and justice, taunting God, dishonoring their parents, hating people, worshipping promiscuity, and lying, to name a few.

We are never too young to stop throwing our lives away and provoking the Lord to his face. Life is a lot easier when we haven't spent the beginning of it destroying as much of it as we can.

Marked by God

Genesis 8:1 says that God "remembered" Noah. The original Hebrew word for "remembered" carries with it a connotation of being marked. The Lord's plan for Noah and his family was more than just to save them from the flood. God marked his man for remembrance to bless him when everyone else had been destroyed. The same word is used in Exodus 2:24 when the Lord remembered his covenant with Abraham, Isaac, and Jacob and began the Exodus.

If we will read the Bible, we will see that he has also marked us for remembrance. God remembers those who trust in his Son, and he will not abandon us. We can take heart in knowing that we are known by the Lord and begin today to be Noah in our families. Maybe your family history is a bleak one, marked by shame and disaster. God can change the course of a family through one man who will set his heart on him.

Following our Father

When the flood waters subsided, the Lord told Noah to "come" out of the ark, in Genesis 8:16. Remember that he had also told Noah to "come into the ark." (Some translations may not use the word "come," but the Hebrew word means to "come.") Throughout Noah's story, God reminds us that he goes before his people. We need to realize that the way has been prepared for us already. Ephesians 2:10 teaches us that we were "created in Christ Jesus for good works, which God prepared beforehand, that we should walk in them" (ESV); we walk the path of righteousness that he has already traveled.

For many men, the fear of the unknown keeps us from completely trusting the Lord. We might worry about what will happen if we fail our families. What if following God costs us our jobs? What if our families don't understand? What if the Lord calls me to do something crazy, like he did with Noah? Just remember, that God always went ahead of Noah. Noah did not go anywhere that the Lord had not already been or do anything that the Lord had not already taken care of. We may lose our jobs; our families may not understand; God may call us to do something crazy. But he has gone before, and the way is ready.

Guidance from Jesus

We have been given a commission much like Noah's. We have been told to build the vehicle in which our families will be saved. And, like Noah, we have been given instructions. These instructions are found throughout the Bible, but for now we will focus on John 14:8–17:5. We don't often think of these three chapters as a guide to the salvation of our families from the wrath of God, but don't just blow through it, because there is a progression of thought throughout the three chapters that teaches us how to live as long as we are here.

This passage includes Jesus' last time sitting down and talking with the disciples before going to the cross, so his words should carry some serious weight for us. For simplicity's sake, we will focus on a few points. As always, it is best to study the passage in its entirety as there is much more to be learned than what will be covered here.

In John 14:8, Philip asks Jesus to help him understand and believe what Jesus is trying to teach the disciples (Jesus is trying to teach them what it means to have faith in him). Jesus answers by telling Philip, "He who has seen me has seen the Father" (NASB). Jesus is telling us that we must trust him and hang our entire world on him. We must begin with faith in the character of God and his Son, Jesus. We cannot build an ark for our families without faith in God's every word. (That's right, every word.) It's not enough to send our kids to church—or even to accompany them—if our lives deny the Word of the Lord.

In verse 15, Jesus extends beyond faith to love. Few things that we do can cause problems for our families as much as if we do not love the Lord. Love should drive our every action. We should tithe, go to work, work hard, and do everything else that we do because we love God. You probably already know that our families can tell when we are doing what we do out of love and when we are not.

The next step that Jesus takes is to teach us that if we love him, we will keep his commandments. We cannot expect to steer our families right and for our homes to be blessed by the Lord if we will not obey him. As much as we may hate the thought, when we disobey God, we are telling him that we know better than he does. We essentially take the reins from his hands.

Ironically, often when we choose to go down the path of disobedience, we do so all the while praying and asking the Lord's blessing. In Psalm 32:9, the Lord admonishes us to "not be as the horse or as the mule which have no understanding, whose trappings include bit and bridle to hold them in check, otherwise they will not come near to you" (NASB). Life is better when God doesn't have to handle us like animals.

As we trust, love, and obey him, we should not fear because he will not leave us as orphans, but will come to us (John 14:18). Noah understood the truth of that promise. While we lead our families, we need to understand that we have not been left to figure it out on our own. To guide our families, our hearts, eyes, ears, and minds have to be set on God. If we build our lives around anything or anyone else, our houses will fall. They will not withstand the storms.

Not only will God be with us, but he will be in us. Jesus teaches that the Holy Spirit will come to live in those who trust him, and that he "will teach you all things, and bring to your remembrance all that [Jesus] said" (John 14:26 NASB). We must learn to "hear," trust, and live according to the Holy Spirit.[3]

There is only one source of truth on which to build our homes. There is only one who has never changed and has never needed to. The truth doesn't have to evolve because it's the truth!

Men want to withstand. We want our children to withstand and to do what's right. There's no other way but to build our families around God and on the truth.

John 15 and 16 primarily contain some of Jesus' last teachings for his disciples. Among the subjects of these teachings is prayer. Throughout his thirty-three years living as one of us (yes, I'm going head-to-head with Joan Osborne theologically), Jesus frequently reminded us of the importance of prayer and showed us by example.

Husbands and daddies, we need to be praying for our families relentlessly. Our guidance for the way we carry out our work responsibilities must come from the Lord. Do you want to provide for your family? Pray. Seek first his kingdom and his righteousness. John 17 finds Jesus praying in the Garden of Gethsemane, knowing that he is about to be arrested, tortured and killed. As he prays, he gives us some wisdom that will help us to keep our minds on him: "This is eternal life, that they may know You, the only true God, and Jesus Christ whom You have sent" (John 17:3 NASB). Because you know God, pray for your families.

Make no mistake, Noah knew the Lord. Even though he may not have known the name of Jesus, he still understood that our righteousness comes from trusting God and trusting God alone. And long after Noah was dead, the Lord provided the sacrifice for Noah's salvation, a sacrifice that Noah had trusted God for. To build our own arks for our families, we must walk in the same way that Noah did and Jesus taught. There is no other way.

By Faith

Now, get ready because we're going to jump again to another place in the Bible that makes no mention of Noah, but teaches us how he lived and was able to build the ark for the salvation of himself and his family.

Romans 7:24–8:11 teaches us more about the life lived by faith, like Noah's life. One of the most common mistakes made by readers of Romans 7 is that we read verses 14–24 and seem to stop there. We tend to read the verses that Paul writes about the struggle between the flesh and the Spirit, and many times we walk away from it thinking something like this: "Well, if Paul struggled against sin and failed most of the time, then I'm doing okay." However, in the words of a strapping young Steven Curtis Chapman from 1990, "You Know Better than That." (That's a line from a song titled "You Know Better than That.") We have to read the Bible as a whole. We cannot stop at verse 24 and pretend that we are not responsible for anything else that God said on the subject.

Verse 24 is the starting point. In order to live by faith, we have to first recognize that we fall hopelessly short in our attempts at righteousness. We are not intended to live in verse 24, even if many Christians around us choose to. The next several verses are a progression that the Lord wants to take us through to save us from the frustration that culminates in verse 24. Think about it. Does verse 24 sound like Noah, Daniel, Shadrach, Meshach, Abednego, Nehemiah, Joseph, or any of the apostles? So, why would we think that God intends us to live there?

Now, don't misunderstand, we all have flesh or human nature, including Noah. Those who have trusted the Lord should not live under its power anymore, though. Romans 7:24 asks, "Who will set me free from the body of this death?" (NASB). The very next verse answers "Thanks be to God through Jesus Christ our Lord" (7:25 NASB)! Because of Jesus, we are free from sin.

Now don't stop there. Keep reading at least through Romans 8:11. We live by faith, not by sight. We should not live to serve our flesh anymore but instead to serve the Spirit of the Lord who lives in us. Most of us have tried our hands at making it on our own. That life led to death, destruction, and heartbreak. Our families do not need us at the helm making decisions according to our flesh. They need us to lead them as we follow God. Our families cannot afford for us to chase our desires anymore (and we can't afford this cost either). We should want our families to be able to say that we love them and that there was never a doubt about that. We should want them to be able to say that we trusted the Lord and that because of him and him alone we were able to stand.

Not by Sight

Noah lived by faith and not by sight. Hebrews 11:5–7 gives us some insight into Noah that we need to keep in mind if we want to be Noahs and to raise Noahs. We established earlier that Noah's father was Lamech, a righteous man, and that his great-grandfather was Enoch, a man commended by the Lord for his faith. Noah's faith was no accident. He was raised in a home where the Word of the Lord was honored. Fathers, it is entirely up to us to decide whether or not his Word will be honored in our homes. Take it or leave it.

Hebrews 11:7a says, "By faith Noah, being warned by God about things not yet seen, in reverence prepared an ark for the salvation of his household" (NASB). We also have been warned of things not yet seen, using the "not yet seen" loosely here because we actually are seeing many of the things we have been warned about taking place. We have been taught in the Bible how to recognize the times and how to see the last days approaching.

We, like Noah, have been told to build an ark for the salvation of our households. Who initiated the building of the ark? God did. He told Noah to build it and how he was to build it. Who sustained the building, the loading of animals, and the voyage of the ark? God did. Our job is to trust him and obey him as we love and nurture our families.

I can't believe that the Lord has given me a household and is filling it with the most amazing wife and three little souls. To be honest, I can let myself be scared to death of making the wrong decisions, of letting something bad happen to my family, and of a million other things. But God has always been the initiator and the sustainer of his work. We need to trust and obey. I don't trust myself to be smart enough, wise enough, strong enough, or anything else enough to be what they need. I do trust the Lord to be all of those things and everything else that they need. The awesome part is that he chooses to be many of those things through us. Set your heart on him and build the ark according to his design.

We are the men who live in these days—days like Noah's. Second Peter 3:3–18 tells us this about the last days: "Know this first of all, that in the last days mockers will come with their mocking, following after their own lusts, and saying, 'Where is the promise of His coming? For ever since the fathers fell asleep, all continues just as it was from the beginning of creation'" (2 Pet. 3:4b NASB). We live in a day when the Word of God is mocked and men work very hard to discredit his Word so that they may follow their own lusts. Not one claim made by the Bible has ever been disproved. In fact, astronomy, geology, archaeology, and yes, even paleontology support the claims made by the Bible, yet we are still being taught Darwinian evolution as established fact in most schools.

Darwinian evolution, as a "theory" has more holes than Swiss cheese at a Texas shooting range. Darwinian evolution does not even qualify as a theory as it is neither testable nor observable. But hey, it wouldn't be the first time that the "scientific" establishment trampled, choked, and possibly even urinated on their own rules to accommodate their best potshot at the Bible. If the scientific community were a *Scrabble* tournament (don't act like you didn't know about those), they'd wake up in the parking lot of the Cheboygan Civic Center with *American Heritage Dictionary* shaped contusions all over their persons.

Not only are the scoffers outside the church. Many ministers, some well-known and well-respected, have publicly denied the inerrancy of the Bible in the name of marketability. "They exchanged the truth of God for a lie, and worshiped and served the creature rather than the Creator" (Rom. 1:25a NASB). In fact, if we will read all of Romans 1, we will see that there is a progression of rebelliousness, which we as a nation have fulfilled to the letter.

If we live in days like Noah's, then as it was in Noah's day, there will come a day when the Lord will shut the door. In Revelation 18:4b, John wrote that he "heard another voice from heaven, saying, 'Come out of her, my people, so that you will not participate in her sins and receive of her plagues'" (NASB). And like Noah, the Lord has told us to build an ark.

Adam

One purpose that Adam serves throughout the Bible is to be a reminder to men that we are responsible for our families. This principle is evident elsewhere in the Bible, such as First Timothy 3:4 where God states that an overseer in the church must be "one who manages his own household well, keeping his children under control with all dignity" (NASB). God has called each of us to some ministry. Whether or not we like to use that word, he intends that we walk in good works that he has prepared in advance for us (Eph. 2:10). As we walk in those good works, we must not lose our families along the way.

Genesis 1:26–30 contains a vital lesson for us that is much like the work of Jim Varney, in that both go criminally overlooked. In these verses, God begins by saying "Let Us make man in Our image, according to Our likeness" (Gen. 1:26 NASB). He goes on to charge man to "fill the earth, and subdue it" (Gen. 1:28 NASB). In essence, man is intended to be like God in every way. That is, not to be equal with God, but to live and continue in his image that we were created in. We were never intended to cultivate our own self-made image. Of course, we are all from different backgrounds, have different tastes and styles, etc. Instead, what God is talking about is that our growth should be toward God and his character, not someone else's. Let's be honest; growing into our own images is killing us.

The people we spend any amount of time with, whether they are family members, co-workers, or even people we only encounter for a moment, should be able to experience the God we serve when they come into contact with us. We should not wonder why we fail and feel ineffective so many times if we are reflecting our own image rather than the one we were created in.

Let's fast-forward to man's first sin, known as "the fall." Once they had sinned and were hiding, God called to Adam for an accounting (Gen. 3:9). Understand from Adam's story that God also comes to us for an accounting for what goes on in our homes. We have to know what is going on in our homes. Our wives and kids have to be able to trust us for that to happen, and knowing is not enough. Sometimes we have to stand in the way of evil when it crouches at the door. Sometimes we have to clean house like Nehemiah and Jesus did. We are the men in our homes. Let's act like it.

In Genesis 3:17–19, the Lord cursed the ground because of sin. He told Adam that he was guilty because he had "heeded the voice of [his] wife" (Gen. 3:17 NKJV) and disobeyed God. Now, Eve received her curses as well, but Adam was held responsible for abdicating his responsibility to his wife. Adam did not step in and put out the fire, so to speak. Instead, he stood by and even participated, following his wife's lead. First Corinthians 11:7 teaches us that man is the "image and glory of God" and that woman is "the glory of man" (NASB). The chapter goes on to speak of man being the head of woman.

Let's stop here and address the questions, concerns, and misgivings that may be rising in your minds. In spite of our "progressive," "enlightened," and "tolerant" thinking (which is clearly making the world a better place, right?), God has established an order to the family. In this order, he has charged the man with the responsibility of leading. These are not my words, but his (see Gen. 2:20–22, 1 Cor. 11:3–12; 1 Tim. 2:11–14; 3:4–5).

We also need to realize that First Corinthians 11:11–12 teaches that woman is not a lesser, subservient partner in a marriage. The Hebrew word for "helper" that God uses to describe Eve in Genesis 2 is also used to describe God in other places in the Old Testament. So, we can safely say that women are not intended by God to be second-class citizens to men. That Hebrew word literally means "to aid" and is derived from a word that means "to surround." To put it simply, man's role is to lead his family as he seeks the guidance of the Lord to do so. The woman's role is to share that calling. Both are to acknowledge God's role and the roles that he designed and blessed for them (1 Cor. 11:11–12).

Now, we can kick and scream about these roles all we want to, but God said what he said, and he knows what he's doing. We absolutely have to stop running from our positions in our families. When you get the chance, listen to what one of the great philosophical minds of the twentieth century, the late Jerry Clower, had to say about feminism.

Several times in the Bible, God holds Adam responsible for the fall. Isaiah 43:27 says, "Your first father sinned" (NKJV).

Romans 5:12 teaches that sin entered the world through "one man" (NASB). First Corinthians 15:22 tells us that "in Adam all die" (NASB). The point is that even though Eve was deceived and ate the fruit first, a point that God acknowledges in First Timothy 2:13-14, God came looking for Adam in the Garden for an accounting. Throughout the Bible, God refers to Adam's sin as the entry point of sin and death into the world.

God does not put us into this position to terrify us. He does not put us into this position to inflate our egos either. He created us to think differently from women. He designed us differently in every way from women. He causes us to function differently emotionally from women. While these differences can create some confusing, albeit entertaining, situations (especially when it's someone else and not you), they were built into us by God himself, by design. Some of the anti-God influences which are prevalent in this world have worked overtime to train these differences out of us. But Jesus once said, "In this world you will have tribulation; but be of good cheer, I have overcome the world" (John 16:33). Considering that we give account for our families, what kind of men ought we to be?

Job

Job "was blameless and upright, and one who feared God and shunned evil" (Job 1:1 NKJV). Job is commended throughout the Bible as a righteous man. One of Job's regular practices was to "rise early in the morning and offer burnt offerings according to the number of" his children (Job 1:5 ESV). "For Job said, 'It may be that my sons have sinned and cursed God in their hearts.' Thus Job did regularly" (Job 1:5 NKJV).

Intercessory prayer for the forgiveness of others is biblical. Job is one example, as are King Hezekiah in Second Chronicles 30, Daniel in Daniel 9, and Jesus on the cross asking forgiveness for those who crucified him. Don't misunderstand, God rightly demands repentance from each of us; however, these prayers were offered by righteous men asking for God's grace and mercy for someone else. God asks the same from us: that we be righteous men praying for his grace and mercy for others. And we know that "the effective, fervent prayer of a righteous man avails much" (James 5:22b NKJV).

We must follow Job's ancient but timeless example in the way that he advocated for his children. Job regularly went to his Father to pray for his children. He routinely put his children and their lives into the hands of God. We have to be men who take our cares for our children to God regularly. How different would the world be if daddies prayed for their kids? How much better would it be if daddies regularly went to the Lord asking for his forgiveness for the sin of his family?

CHAPTER 2

Do what's Right, the Right Way, for the Right Reasons because they're Watching

WITHOUT QUESTION, WE have to do the right things if we want to be useful to God, to our families, and to the other people around us. But it's not enough to do what's right; we have to do it the right way. You guessed it; we also need to do the right things the right way for the right reasons. What is the reason that we should do the things we do? According to First Corinthians 13:1–3, the answer is love. Anything that we can do, apart from love, is worthless.

Love has an enemy in our world. We live in a world that preaches tolerance. Look what tolerance has done to us. What secular society calls "tolerance" is in fact the treating of all views and ideas as potentially true, except for views and ideas that are true, of course. This brand of tolerance allows people to avoid discussing serious issues and problems, especially issues with an obvious solution. The best part about this tolerance is that it is militantly and oppressively forced upon us in every aspect of our lives.

Tolerance will let you live, but it will also let you die. But, love will save your life. Tolerance will ignore your self-destructive behavior. (Thank you, mama and daddy, for not being tolerant.) Love will leave its own comfort behind to seek and save the soul who has wandered into harm's way. Our world is dying for love. Those of us who know the Lord and trust him with our lives have what they need. In all the examples that follow, love is the common theme. In the name of love, we have to run counter to the current of pseudo-tolerance.

Men of Issachar

In First Chronicles 12:32, we find a group of men who did the right thing at a dangerous time. At that point in history, God had rejected Saul as king of Israel and had sent Samuel to anoint David as king in his place. The jealous Saul sought to kill David and keep the throne. For years, David had to hide from Saul. But every time David had an opportunity to kill Saul, he refused. David would not "stretch out [his] hand against the Lord's anointed" (1 Sam. 26:9 NKJV).

David hid in Hebron during those times. While he was there, some Israelites began to leave Saul and join David, recognizing him as God's anointed. Now, to openly leave the sitting king and offer allegiance to another would have been a death sentence. But these men did the right thing. Living by sight and not by faith, it would have looked safer to stay with the sitting king, but these men did what was right anyway. And one group in particular is singled out specifically because they did the right thing for the right reason.

The Bible says that "the sons of Issachar" were "men who understood the times, with knowledge of what Israel should do"

(1 Chron. 12:32 NASB). Of all of the groups listed in the chapter who left Saul to recognize and support David as king, these men were recorded as understanding the times and knowing what Israel should do.

How can we understand the times and know what we should do? We can do it the same way they did it. Romans 12:2 tells us not to "be conformed to this world," but to "be transformed by the renewing of [our minds], that [we] may prove what the will of God is" (NASB). We must not be conformed to this world. The man of this world is a liar, unfaithful, selfish, unloving, weak (but profoundly convinced of his own strength), and concerned with his own satisfaction. The results of these men filling the void left by real men are devastating. With God's help, we need to look at ourselves with "sober" judgment, as the next verse (Rom. 12:3) prescribes, and understand whether or not we conform to this world.

Instead, our minds must be renewed so that we may be transformed into what the Lord wants us to be. Our thinking, judgment, and perceptions must be changed to those of God. Now the staunch atheist/humanist/secularist will say, "Aha! I knew it! He wants me to deny reason and for all people to become robots who all think the same way!" To this, the appropriate response would be: "First of all, calm down. Second, the Lord gave us reason and logic, and their employment will invariably lead to an acknowledgement of the truth, namely that he is God and his thinking is right. Finally, the Lord has made us all different. He only asks that we be like-minded in that we all accept his Word as truth and that we live according to his Word in faith."

Once the men of Issachar discerned what God was doing, they did the right thing the right way and for the right reason. We have to be willing to do the same. Our children are watching us. Our co-workers are watching us. Some of them are looking for encouragement and strength. Some of them are searching for truth. Some of them want to see us falter. They all need to see nothing less than God himself in the lives that we live.

Proverbs 22:6

"Train up a child in the way he should go, even when he is old he will not depart from it" (NASB). The Hebrew word translated "train up" literally means to "narrow," "initiate," and "discipline." The Bible teaches parents to raise their children, disciplining them and training them up in the way they should go. Fathers are admonished not to exasperate their children (Col. 3:21). Psalm 127, among other Psalms and Proverbs, teaches that children are gifts from the Lord. The Bible is full of examples of parents teaching and being instructed to teach their children the Word of God to guide their lives.

Now, trouble arises when we see parents around us seemingly doing these things but not achieving the desired results. Could it even happen to me or to you? One of the most unbearable thoughts in the mind of a father is the fear that he might fail his family and drive them away from the Lord.

First things first, we must begin by completely entrusting our parenting to God alone. Let's be honest: we all have a past. Let's be really honest: we all have a present. One of my greatest fears is that my family will suffer because of my faults. The Lord has an answer to those fears. He asks that we trust him. There is no other way to overcome our pasts than repentance. We cannot cover it up. We cannot pretend it never happened. We absolutely cannot expect the Lord to bless our families and our homes if we will not acknowledge him and trust him with our sin. Whatever is in our pasts, the Lord is ready to forgive, and he is able to bless our families.

In Second Kings 18 and 19, the Bible records a great moment

in history. The whole story won't be related here, but we should pay attention to one specific point. When the Assyrian field commander threatened King Hezekiah, he listed other kingdoms that had fallen, whose gods had not been able to save them from his hand. In Second Kings 19:14–19, Hezekiah took the threatening letter to the temple and spread it out before the Lord. In his prayer he acknowledges that other kingdoms had fallen to the Assyrians. Hezekiah understood why they fell. Their trust was in everything except the Lord. Hezekiah abandoned every other option and put his faith in God alone.

Hezekiah set us an example that we must follow if we want to see our families saved. When other families around us fall, even other Christian families, we have to take the threats of this world and of our own sin to God and spread them out before him. We can trust him without reservation because he is ready to forgive and to strengthen those who trust him.

Too many Christian parents honor God verbally and in certain areas of their lives, but display a disregard for his Word in other parts of their lives. We see parents who neither show honor to the Sabbath nor consistently involve themselves as members of a church. We see parents who simply do not trust the Lord with their work. We see parents showing more concern for their "rights" to do what makes them happy than for the well-being of their children and other people in their lives. Now there are many parents all around us who are obeying God in these areas. But we must acknowledge the connection between the behavior of many Christian parents in recent times and the change in our culture.

Very few things will turn children away from the Lord like hypocrisy in their parents. If we won't be the men in our homes, then who will? Only one person has been appointed by God to be the fence post in your home.

The family that honors the Lord stands opposed to the work

of Satan in the world. If we want to raise our families to know the Lord in a world where we have targets on our backs, then there is no other way than to train up our children in the way that they should go. Daddies, the Word of God must be our first and final authority in everything. As our final authority, we must honor and obey his Word without exception. If we think we know better than God when it comes to church attendance, creation, tithing, sex, marriage, money, speech, time, or (fill in this blank with anything you like), then we should expect our kids to do the same. Be a man. Raise your kids.

Daniel, Shadrach, Meshach, and Abednego

Four men who always stand out in my mind as fence posts are found in the book of Daniel. These four men are the embodiment of doing the right things, the right way, for the right reason. Taken from their homes and families at a young age; witnessing the strength of their nation crushed, humiliated, and devastated; relocated to Babylon, the belly of the beast; and ordered to serve the king, Daniel, Shadrach, Meshach and Abednego made a decision. These four young men made up their minds.

We know from Daniel 1:3 that these four were Hebrew nobles, possibly even royals (not of the Kansas City variety), but everything they had and could have had was snatched away when Babylon took Judah. However, they were given an opportunity to regain a highly coveted status in Babylon if they would play by Babylon's rules.

Verse four records that these young men were given a good Babylonian education. Now, attention to current events and a study of history will show that controlling education, especially from a young age, is one of the most effective ways to steer the direction of an entire culture. Adolf Hitler infamously boasted in a speech in 1933 that "your child belongs to us already," in reference to his influence over the public education system.[4] These four promising young men would have to be "educated" in order to get them to buy-in to becoming good Babylonians. But Daniel would be the one, by virtue of being exalted by God, who would be educating the wise men of Babylon.

In verse five, we learn that they would also be fed the same food that the king himself ate. They would be well taken care of, but they would have to forsake what postmodernists would call "their own personal beliefs" to stay in such good graces. We are urged every day to play by this world's rules. Bumper stickers admonish us to "coexist," and the implication is that we do so by profaning the Son of God by declaring him to be no different from Mohammed, secular humanism, Buddha, or anything else that man comes up with in an effort to escape the acknowledgment of God.

We are told, often even from within "Christian" circles, that church attendance, biblical tithing, biblical marriage, biblical creation, biblical parenting, and biblical morality are not "viable" in our culture. Pray for mercy for these people as you continue to trust the Lord rather than people who are bent on their own destruction.

As insurance for the Babylonians, Daniel 1:7 tells us that they even changed the names of our four heroes. Now, why would anyone want to do a thing like that? Did they just not like the Hebrew names? No, there was something much more sinister at work. Our names carry our identities. Each of us was born with a name. Some of us have to live our names down. Some work to maintain or even live up to a good family name. When the Babylonian official gave them new names, he essentially attempted to change their identities. They were no longer to be Hebrew nobles but instead to become subservient to Babylon, receiving their names, food, and education from a godless nation.

Given those circumstances, these young men had already made up their minds to honor the Lord rather than the guilty king. They did it the right way, and respectfully honored God, putting their own necks on the line, and no one else's. They did it for the right reason: they knew God, and nothing less would ever be good enough again. Because they honored the Lord, the great Nebuchadnezzar, king of Babylon, took notice, and the road was paved for the rest of the book of Daniel to unfold.

Daniel and his friends taught us another valuable lesson in Daniel chapter two. This lesson is particularly important for fathers. Chapter two recounts Nebuchadnezzar's troubling dream and his search for someone who could tell him the dream's meaning. He even went so far as to decree that any of his wise men who could not interpret the dream would be brutally executed and their homes burned.

Verses 17–18 contain Daniel's reaction to the news, and it is nothing short of beautiful. "Then Daniel went to his house, and made the decision known to Hananiah, Mishael, and Azariah, his companions, that they might seek mercies from the God of heaven concerning this secret, so that Daniel and his companions might not perish with the rest of the wise men of Babylon" (NKJV).

The word "friends" is used here and nowhere else in the book of Daniel. There were many wise men in the kingdom, but Daniel chose to spend his time with Shadrach, Meshach and Abednego, and call them "friends." Who do you call friend? Are your friends the kind of people you can call and pray with if your life was on the line? Are you that kind of friend to them?

When the most powerful man in the world, by man's standards, assured their deaths, these friends did not run; it was not "every man for himself." They followed the precedent that they had already established in their lives. They prayed. God, recognizing the familiar voices of his children in distress, answered. (See Psalm 18 or Second Samuel 22 for further reading.)

This lesson is an important one for daddies because, like Daniel and his friends did, we set precedents. We set them for our families. Set the right ones. We have to establish that in our homes the Word of God is final and takes precedence over anything else.

They need to know that daddy knows the Lord and lives by his Word. They need to know that money and everything else material belongs to God. They need to know what marriage and love are because they've seen them up close, and they don't know anything different. They shouldn't even have a frame of reference for unfaithfulness or the thought of divorce. They need to know that it's right to be the same person in private and public, on Sunday morning and Saturday night, and at work or school or in your own room. They need to know that because their daddy has lived this way every day of their lives. They need to know that they are more important to the man in their lives than his career goals.

The Lord provides us an example for this kind of living. Because Daniel and his friends had been established by the Lord, they were able to stand and not falter in a kingdom that was hostile to people who were faithful to God. The Bible does not record how long Shadrach, Meshach and Abednego lived, but we do know that at least Daniel survived the entire 70-year Babylonian exile. During that time, he lived under the rules of at least three monarchs. Each of those kings took office with an apparent determination to elevate himself over all other gods (sometimes with particular attention to the God of the Israelites), and every time, the God of the Israelites stood in the way. And God blocked the paths of these kings using four

Hebrew men who did what was right, the right way and (you guessed it) for the right reasons. Of the three Babylonian kings in the book of Daniel, two acknowledged God, and one died because he would not.

Nebuchadnezzar was accustomed to bringing all of the peoples of the world into submission under his power. But four young men wouldn't eat his food for no other reason than the command of their God. They laid their lives down to honor his Word. (But God picked their lives back up because there were a couple of other kings who still needed to meet him.)

These young men also refused to go through the motions and worship an image of Nebuchadnezzar so that they could live, so Nebuchadnezzar commanded that they be executed. But the most powerful man on earth's orders to execute, carried out to the letter, failed to execute. And he was allowed to see what went wrong with his plan; the Lord was in the furnace with his men. Finally, Nebuchadnezzar, one of the greatest movers and shakers in the history of the world, had no choice but to acknowledge God.

For Daniel, it all started over again when Belshazzar was in charge. Belshazzar went out of his way to provoke the one God, as do many modern atheists and humanists, and he died for his defiance. Belshazzar's story demonstrates that, once again, the Lord upholds lone men doing the right things, and through these men, even a king cannot run from God.

That very night a new king, Darius, took the kingdom from Belshazzar. Once again, the Lord took care of his servant Daniel. God caused the three most powerful men on earth to acknowledge him before his servant Daniel's eyes. Because Daniel did the right things, the right way, and for the right reasons, he not only witnessed these miracles, but was used by the Lord to bring them about.

As with Daniel, God wants his men today to stand and

do what's right in a land that is hostile and seeks to discredit, silence, and eliminate the voice of the Lord. And like Daniel, we will stand if we trust the one God and his Word as our final authority. And like Daniel, as we stand, the world around us will have no choice but to acknowledge the Lord, as Jesus said in Matthew 5:16, "Let your light shine before men in such a way that they may see your good works, and glorify your Father who is in heaven" (NASB).

Our Families are Watching

I spent a few years in my twenties playing in a band with some of my best friends. We made Christian music, much of which was written by two of the guys in the band who were tremendously musically talented. During our travels, adventures, and shenanigans, we met and got to know many other bands and musicians, all of whom proclaimed a message in their music, their behavior, and their interactions with the people around them. One of the most prevalent themes that musicians communicated was animosity toward parents. It got really weird when the objects of this animosity were in attendance, lending support to the musical pursuits of their whiny children, thereby rendering the faux outrage impotent.

As a high school teacher, I have often heard similar expressions of frustration and even hatred from the mouths of children directed at their parents. As a parent, myself, I often wonder how parents and children get to places where that type of resentment exists. The natural next thought is "Am I leading my family down the same path?" The answer to that question lies with our Wonderful Counselor and Everlasting Father, and he teaches us by example once again.

Joshua established that he and his family would serve the Lord (Josh. 24:15). But saying it is never enough; Joshua unequivocally lived those words out. In the same way, declaring that our families are servants of God is not enough. In fact, one of the quickest ways to embitter children and to cause them to resent their parents and their training is for those parents to honor God with their lips when their hearts are far from him.

Instead, the Bible commands us to teach our children to honor the Lord. Psalm 34:11 says, "Come, you children, listen to me; I will teach you the fear of the Lord" (NASB). When we call our children near to teach them the fear of the Lord, do they know by our lives that we mean what we say? Is it a painful joke to them when their parents try to teach them to honor the same Word of God that they wink at and "interpret" when it serves their purposes? Our ruthless enemy works hard to destroy our families and will not spare our children, given the chance. But the Lord is able to save and to keep both them and us. Have you trusted the Almighty God with your children? Have you trusted him with your own life? Are you raising them according to his Word?

If you're a young father and you think like most of us do, then you'll be asking the same question that Psalm 119:9 asks: "How can a young man cleanse his way?" (NKJV). The same verse answers, "By taking heed according to Your word" (NKJV). If we want to be the kind of men that our children can take seriously when we teach them the fear of the Lord, then we must keep our lives according to his Word. That life will never be possible without his Holy Spirit living in us, and we must live according to the Holy Spirit instead of according to our own human nature, which the Bible calls "the flesh." Life according to the Spirit must be more tangible than a lofty goal, or else the fight is already lost.

In disciplining our children, we need wisdom. The Bible teaches us in Ephesians 6:4 not to "provoke [our] children to anger; but bring them up in the discipline and instruction of the

Lord" (NASB). Colossians 3:21 further clarifies this principle by teaching us not to "exasperate [our] children, so that they will not lose heart" (NASB). Disciplining our children is clearly commanded throughout the Bible, but how can we be certain that we will not provoke our children to anger or exasperate them?

Often, people see the angry and rebellious children mentioned earlier and chalk it up to negligent parents; however, many times, the attitudes and beliefs of such children are the result of parents who worked very hard to discipline them and raise them right, and tragically, they went too far too often, provoking their children to anger and exasperating them. Now that we're all sufficiently panicked, fear not. God has taken it upon himself to provide us an example.

In Isaiah 57:15–16, the Everlasting Father reveals his thoughts to us concerning discipline. The verses read:

> For thus says the High and Lofty One Who inhabits eternity, whose name is Holy, "I dwell in the high and holy place, with him who has a contrite and humble spirit, to revive the spirit of the humble, and to revive the heart of the contrite ones. For I will not contend forever, nor will I always be angry; for the spirit would fail before Me, and the souls which I have made." (NKJV)

God dwells "on a high and holy place," and so must we. We cannot effectively discipline our children from a position of hypocrisy. If we try to, then resentment will be the natural result.

God also dwells "with the contrite and humble spirit, to revive the spirit of the humble, and to revive the heart of the contrite ones" (Isa. 57:15 NKJV). When our children are contrite and lowly in spirit because of their sin or for any other reason, we need to be close to them and to revive their spirits and their hearts by comforting and encouraging them. They need to be assured of our unwavering love for them. If we refuse our children's repentance, then we will crush them. We will push them elsewhere to find illegitimate means to express their love and find release from the guilt we've heaped upon them.

Simultaneously being in a high and holy place and with the contrite and lowly is a miracle that God not only does for us, but wants to demonstrate through us, as parents. Hebrews 4:15 teaches that our high priest, Jesus, is not "a high priest who cannot sympathize with our weaknesses" (NASB). We must follow his example and sympathize with our children's weaknesses. Sympathizing does not mean condoning or ignoring, but rather understanding that overcoming human nature is difficult. In fact, overcoming human nature by human means is impossible. "However, you are not in the flesh but in the Spirit, if indeed the Spirit of God dwells in you" (Rom. 8:9a NASB).

Isaiah revealed that if God contended forever and was perpetually angry, "the spirit would fail" before him and "the souls which [he has] made" (Isa. 57:16 NKJV). The discipline of the Lord, like all good discipline, hurts. But he does not utterly crush us. In the true love of a father, he disciplines his children to teach them to respect the boundary between right and wrong. And in the true love of a father, he recognizes repentance and brokenness and revives his children's hearts and spirits. Contrary to much of modern parenting theory, the greatest example for you to follow is the discipline of your Father.

CHAPTER 3

Love Your Wife

Loving our wives has always been important and always will be important. Our love for our wives sets the precedent and the frame of reference for everyone else in our lives, especially our children, to understand love and to understand God. To deviate from the Lord's commands concerning marriage and our love for our wives is to misrepresent him and his character to those around us. And, yes, as men we do set the precedents for those around us, in our homes, workplaces, churches, and anywhere else.

This concept is not a sexist belittling of women. There are some things that men can do better than women, and there are some things that women can do better than men. This is the design of God himself, and I would contend that to belittle that truth or to deny the differences between men and women based on the assumption that being different must necessarily mean being unequal is suggestive of sexism.

The love of a husband for his wife has been mocked, marginalized, and belittled for centuries, but in recent decades, we have witnessed a surge in the intensity of these attacks. Many prominent figures in our popular culture, academia, and social movements have all worked in concert to undermine the importance of the family.

Many popular TV shows have incrementally increased their efforts to belittle good men and to glamorize, romanticize and normalize divorce, promiscuity, unwed parenthood, and homo/trans-sexuality. Of course, some voices still speak the truth in our culture, but many are undeniably pushing to destroy the family.

One example is Disney Channel's 2010–2014 children's sitcom *Good Luck Charlie,* which saw fit to present as normal to our children a family with two mothers. In an interview with *TV Guide,* a Disney spokesperson disclosed that the episode was "developed under the consultancy of child development experts and community advisors," and was "developed to be relevant to kids and families around the world and to reflect themes of diversity and inclusiveness."[5] The consultants were undisclosed. To lend her support to Disney's decision, the model of sexual wholesomeness, Miley Cyrus, tweeted, "I commend Disney for making this step into the light of this generation. They control so much of what kids think!"[6]

Another example comes to us from ABC in the form of the sitcom *Modern Family.* ABC's *Modern Family* website describes the show as "culturally defining."[7] The series features the Pritchett family wherein father and husband Jay Pritchett is married to his "young, vivacious second wife, Gloria, who resists his old-fashioned ways."[8] The website does not specify which of his ways are "old-fashioned," but among his ways is an uneasiness with his son's homosexual relationship, which is characterized as "loving" by the series website. Implicit in the title, *Modern Family,* is the idea that it is normal in most families for loving homosexual children to have to exercise patience with their "old-fashioned" fathers' discomfort with their decisions.

Not to be outdone, NBC made an effort to normalize the

perversion of the family with *The New Normal*, which was roundly rejected by viewers (there were easily tens of them). NBC's *The New Normal* website begins by proclaiming, "These days, families come in all forms—single dads, double moms, sperm donors, egg donors, one-night-stand donors. . . . It's 2012 and anything goes."[9] The show features a homosexual couple who want to have a baby, but for reasons that are apparently beyond humanity's ability to comprehend, cannot. The answer to their supplications to no specific deity (because to specify one would be sexist, or racist, or hate speech, or something) comes in the form of Goldie, who becomes the surrogate mother. Goldie is "a Midwestern waitress and single mother looking to escape her dead-end life and a small-minded grandmother."[10] What makes the grandmother small-minded? She does not approve of homosexuality. Once again, the title of the show itself creates the false narrative that homosexuality is, well, normal. Oh, and don't miss the potshot at Middle America, courtesy of our moral betters in Hollywood.

Let's not forget one of the most successful sitcoms of the nineties, NBC's *Friends*. The wildly popular series featured a group of six single friends sleeping with anything that they could get close to. These "normal 20–30-year-olds" spent their days and nights demonstrating the self-control and moral discernment of a randy chimpanzee. They slept with their boyfriends/girlfriends, each other's boyfriends/girlfriends, other people's boyfriends, girlfriends, spouses, and even perfect strangers (not to be confused with Larry Appleton and Balki Bartokomous; they were better than that). Oh, but they had standards. Whenever one of them was the victim of infidelity, they made moral judgments and sought vengeance. But if one of them made an honest mistake (and who hasn't, right?), it was treated as nothing more than a punch line.

In May of 2013, the NBA's Jason Collins came out of the

closet, receiving praise from President Obama for his courage. On the same day, Army Sgt. First Class Craig Robinson completed Air Assault School on a prosthetic leg, a first time feat described by Lt. Col. Allen West as "the toughest 10 days in the Army."[11] Robinson, who lost the leg in military service, had to repair the broken prosthetic twice during the trial, and still met the same standard as every able-bodied man. There was no acknowledgment from the president.

On the night of June 26, 2015 the White House was lit up with the colors of the rainbow to hail the Supreme Court ruling legalizing same-sex "marriage" across the nation. Once again, our president showed tremendous class as he handled a highly controversial and divisive issue.

And who could forget Bruce Jenner's transition into "Caitlyn?" The metamorphosis culminated in his being awarded ESPN's courage award for the year of 2015. Jenner was deemed more worthy of the award than Mt. St. Joseph basketball player Lauren Hill, who stayed on and played with her team after having been diagnosed with terminal brain cancer.

These are just a few examples of an effort by a loud few to push an agenda to undermine the family, as designed by God. A postmodern culture believes that the roles of men and women are not a calling and a responsibility, but a constraining construct of religious zealots. They don't want real men around, until confronted by real danger or until their hip, enlightened, postmodern "men" run out on them and leave them hurt, abandoned, and scrambling to pick up the pieces. Then, they wonder whatever happened to real men.

Men's roles have also been an important target for critical theorists. Critical theory was born out of the Frankfurt School, which was born out of Marxism. The ultimate goal of communism is a world ruled by one government. They don't like to use the word "ruled," but let's be honest; when an all-powerful entity governs every aspect of the lives of a voiceless people, what else can it be called? Communism's natural enemy is freedom. Freedom is upheld by morality. Many of America's founding fathers understood this principle, wrote about it, and spoke about it. (If you don't believe me, read their writings. They're some of the best-kept secrets in the world.)

In order to topple freedom, America must be fundamentally transformed. In order for America to be fundamentally transformed, two things have to happen: morality must be undermined and the free people must be made willing to give their liberty away. Critical theory was created to accomplish both of those ends. And one of its favorite targets is the family, and more specifically, the head of the family.

Rebellious human nature lends itself to the undermining of morality, as demonstrated in the Garden of Eden where the serpent tempted Eve by questioning God's command and the motives behind it. Out of this desire of our human nature sprang Deconstructionism, a model of thinking that allows for no certainty other than the certainty that nothing is certain, seriously. Deconstructionism remains popular amongst communists, agnostics, and frat boys "looking to score."

The prevalent use of deconstruction as the weapon of choice for those who seek to do away with morality is one important reason why we as men must know what we believe and why we believe it. And there's no better way than to seek the truth by seeking the Lord. Seeking the truth is not enough; we must move to align ourselves with the truth. That is one important difference between a fence post man and any other man: while others move the truth to fit their beliefs, we move our beliefs to fit the truth. The truth has never moved and never will.

Even if morality were completely obliterated, how could a free people be persuaded to give their liberties away? History answers that question for us. People willingly give their liberties over to a government when they are convinced or "re-educated" to believe that the nation, which has historically operated under those freedoms, has done harm to the rest of the world. The people must also become divided against each other to marginalize and even eliminate those who recognize and oppose the erosion of freedom. Groups who believe that they have been victimized by another group have historically relinquished their freedoms to governments who have promised social justice (this is just a code word for revenge). We see these same principles at work in America today, and the second and third waves of feminism (and arguably some aspects of the first) target men who love their wives.

The feminist movement was not borne out of critical theory, but marries with it nicely and has been adopted as one of its pillars. Feminism relies upon the acceptance of several fallacious assumptions. The average feminist holds one or more of the following beliefs: every aspect of western culture has been designed by men for men and does not afford women the same opportunities as men, marriage was instituted by men to oppress women, women should "enjoy" promiscuity in order to experience fulfillment, and that men are animals who cannot control sexual impulses. They may also believe that Beyonce Knowles is empowering women by taking every opportunity to publicly degrade her body, being married to a man whose song lyrics have historically been misogynistic, and by recording a song called "Bow Down" wherein she calls on young girls who aspire to be like her to "bow down, b!@#$%s." The song goes on from there to explain that, yes, she is married, but it's not what you think.

Modern third-wave feminism's main objective is to liberate women from perceived oppression. So, what's the harm in letting some misguided women pursue their dreams? They're only hurting themselves, right? Well, not exactly. A feminist must necessarily reject God's moral law as spelled out in the Bible. The feminist rejects God's establishment of equally important roles for men and women. The average feminist rejects the Lord's intended purpose and safeguards for sex.

When these beliefs enter into a household, they will destroy that household. If we do not take some biblical morals seriously, then why should we care about any of them? In the absence of morals, self-preservation and self-gratification become law. Natural law dictates that the pursuit of self-preservation and self-gratification results in divorce, depression, higher incidences of drug problems for children, and even suicide.

The solution has been taught to us since the beginning of time. The solution is a man who honors the Lord and loves his family. All of the "intellectual" feminist, critical theorist, and popular philosophical arguments in the world cannot stand against a good man who knows and honors the Lord.

What is Love? (Baby, Don't Hurt Me. Just Kidding—Seriously, Though, Don't.)

As a high school English teacher, I get to hear the thoughts of teenagers from a broad cross-section of our society. Many of the literary works that we study deal with love as a major theme, so the class discussions get interesting/funny/alarming. Every year I am amazed at the number of students who hold the belief that love is an emotion or a feeling. I have been asked, "Why don't Romeo and Juliet just divorce?" or, "Why does Sydney Carton promise Lucie that he will never speak of his love for her again?" or, "Why do we have to address you as 'Biff Stonebreaker'?" These questions arise from an ignorance as to what love is. We have to welcome these questions because they are ripe opportunities to present the truth to those who want to know what love is—like Foreigner.

As always, the Bible is the first and final authority on the subject. When the Lord talks about love, he usually talks about what love does, as in First John 4:10, Ephesians 5:25, John 14:15, and First Corinthians 13, to name a few instances. And, in a nutshell, what love does is what is best for its object. Christ loved the church and gave himself up for her (Eph. 5:25). In John 14:15, Jesus said "If you love Me, you will keep My commandments" (NASB). First John 4:10 says "In this is love, not that we loved God, but that he loved us and sent His Son to be the propitiation for our sins" (NASB). Everything listed in First Corinthians 13 that love is or does is an act of selflessness.

For all of these biblical teachings about love to be true, love cannot possibly be an emotion or a circumstance-based attraction. And, for the evolutionary adherents out there, love is not a condition of compatibility between the pheromones and hormones of a male and a female specimen of the same species. In fact, for that compatibility to have evolved we would have to accept that the necessary organs and their functions would have to have evolved simultaneously in structure as well as function. If that's not ridiculous enough, evolution from asexual reproduction to sexual reproduction would dramatically decrease the rate of success. So, natural selection would have selected traits that work against the survival of the organism.

The biblical teachings about love leave only one possibility: love is a decision and a commitment, a "decitment" if you will (and I will). A commitment, at its essence, is unbreakable. Here we see the diametric opposition of the world's definition of love and God's. We also see one of the reasons that he urges his people not to divorce, as it is a misrepresentation of marriage, love, and God himself.

Now that we have established what love is biblically (and nothing else really matters), why is it so important for a man to love his wife? When a man loves his wife, he establishes a secure home base for his family that is a type and a shadow of God's love for his people. The children in such a household can know that their father will come home after work instead of running around on their mother. They can know that their mother rests in the knowledge that the man of the house is always the same man. Everyone in the home has a frame of reference for not only staying together, but working for each other's good, instead of the precedent of leaving or being left (physically or emotionally) when "it's not working" anymore.

A great representation of this principle can be found in the 1968 movie *Yours, Mine and Ours*. I have still never seen the entire movie, so I can't vouch for it, but I caught the end of it once and was very impressed with the scene when Helen goes into labor. The scene takes place late at night. Chaos ensues as several unrelated crises converge on the one inconvenient moment. As Frank helps his wife to the car, he's putting out fires right and left. Along the way, he counsels his daughter about what love is. He explains it by saying "Look around you," referencing the family's reliance on and consideration for each other in the difficult situation. Love is neither defined nor evidenced by how it feels, but by what it does. Feelings can be fun, but feelings can also be fickle and fleeting. What would your kids say that love is?

Marry Right

Now that we know what love is, let's talk about pre-emptive measures. Statistically, most divorces are attributed to matters of sex, money, and social media (a recent phenomenon); however, I want to suggest that most of the problems take place before sex, money, social media or anything else even have a chance to cause problems. This problem is laid out in Psalm 127:1, "Unless the Lord builds the house, they labor in vain who build it; unless the Lord guards the city, the watchman stays awake in vain." We cannot choose who and when to marry better than the God who created us. No matter how much we plan and try to safeguard against the pitfalls that ensnare so many others, only God can sustain a marriage as it should be.

It is a well-known generalization that a woman will often marry a man with the intention of changing him; however, many men have been guilty of the same error. Many marriages end in divorce or lead to very unhappy and unhealthy homes because the Lord was not the one who constructed the home.

"But what if I'm already married? What if I already made a mistake and my marriage is in trouble?" The answer to this entire problem can be found in Psalm 32:6-9:

> For this cause everyone who is godly shall pray to You in a time when you may be found; surely in a flood of great waters they shall not come near him. You are my hiding place; You shall preserve me from trouble; You shall surround me with songs of deliverance. Selah.
>
> I will instruct you and teach you in the way you should go; I will guide you with My eye. Do not be like the horse or like the mule, which have no understanding, which must be harnessed with bit and bridle, else they will not come near you. (NKJV)

Now, these verses are about pre-empting, heading off potential problems before they have a chance to arise. Before marriage is the time of finding out. The Lord is trying to guide us and spare us from the misery and suffering that come from seeking our own illegitimate fulfillment. Are you listening to him? If we will allow him to build our homes, then the "flood of great waters" won't reach us. Will there still be difficult times in life and even within our homes? Absolutely, but they will not sink the man whose house has been built by the Lord. "You shall surround me with songs of deliverance" (Ps. 32:7 NKJV). Do you hear that? Those are the Words of God himself to you. Trust him with whom you will (and will not) marry. Trust him with the way you love your wife. Trust him with the upbringing of the children he has given you.

Don't be like an animal that has to be led by a bit and bridle. Life is much more fun when we willingly follow God. If he says no, then gratefully understand that he has spared you from what you would have done on your own.

For those who may already have married, and done so against the direction of the Lord, it's not too late (no, divorce is not the answer). Let's back up in Psalm 32; verses 1–5 hold the answer:

> How blessed is he whose transgression is forgiven, whose sin is covered! How blessed is the man to whom the Lord does not impute iniquity, and in whose spirit there is no deceit! When I kept silent about my sin, my body wasted away through my groaning all day long. For day and night Your hand was heavy upon me; my vitality was drained away as with the fever heat of summer. Selah.
>
> I acknowledged my sin to You, and my iniquity I did not hide; I said, "I will confess my transgressions to the Lord"; and You forgave the guilt of my sin. Selah. (NASB)

Now, let's be honest. If we went against the direction of the Lord and married someone we should not have, that was wrong. I understand that's not a romantic thought, and acknowledging that wrong to your wife may not be a fun conversation. But if you're serious about wanting God's blessing back in your marriage, then there is no other way.

Blessing and joy are found in the confession of our sin to the Lord (Ps. 32:1–2). When our spirits are free from the deceit of justifying our sin, we can be forgiven in the eyes of God. Trying to live in denial of our sin is miserable, plain and simple (Ps. 32:3–4). We were never meant to live that way. Trying to atone for our wrongs on our own and in our own ways is miserable and will leave us bitter old men.

But we don't have to end up that way. A seemingly (or actually) failed marriage is not hopeless. In fact, God has been known to be in the business of saving the hopeless. The psalmist wants us to know that he was forgiven once he brought everything to the Lord (Ps. 32:5). The same is true for us. I can't promise you an overnight fix to all of your problems. You and I have still done the things we've done, forgiven or not. What I can promise, because God has promised it, is that he will forgive any man who confesses his sin and trusts the Lord with his life, including the wrong he has done.

I have seen God take marriages that began in rebellion of one kind or another, and save them. He saved those marriages when the people in them acknowledged their sin and turned to him for hope. Sometimes it starts with only one spouse. It may not be easy, but it beats the alternative every single time.

It's Not about You

One of the most disgusting and destructive aspects of our culture is the entitled mindset. The religion of self is pushed upon us at every turn. Some employees believe that pay is merited simply because they showed up to work. We are told things like "chase your dreams" and "follow your heart." Many people marry in hopes of finding fulfillment. Most of these same people also leave the marriage in hopes of finding fulfillment. Many parents' lives suggest that they don't really want to be parents.

(I have heard parents use the phrase "me time" with a straight face.) The insatiable appetite for self is often romanticized in our literature and movies and has been viewed this way, to some degree, for a long time.

When we follow our hearts and do what makes us happy, we're not only being selfish, we're being unwise. Jeremiah 17:9 characterizes our hearts accurately when the Lord says: "The heart is more deceitful than all else and is desperately sick; who can understand it?" (NASB). In essence, what we want can often get us into trouble. The pursuit of what we want can often hurt those around us. Men who live for themselves often leave their families, either physically or emotionally. And, we all know the results of an absentee man of the house. These men leave their children with nothing but his tarnished name and a void that will be filled by an alternative. Our culture is eager to provide many alternatives, none of them good. When a man has the mindset that he is owed something, or that his happiness is even as important as the well-being of his family, then he has introduced a deadly cancer into his home.

During my older sister's engagement, we went one day to visit our great-grandparents. As we sat at the kitchen table, our great-grandmother began to talk to my sister about marriage. Our great-grandparents married and had loved each other faithfully for sixty-four years. So when she talked about marriage, we listened. She told her soon-to-be married great-granddaughter that, "a lot of people say that in marriage, everything's 50/50. Well, it's not. It's 100/100." She was right. We cannot go into marriage thinking that our wives will have to meet us halfway. We have to give ourselves for our wives, just as Jesus did for his bride, the church. Nothing less is acceptable. Here we have to do some soul searching. If you're not willing to go that far, then marriage may not be for you. And the Bible teaches that there's nothing wrong with being single. It's better to have no marriage than a wrong one.

Treat Her Right and See What Happens

Chips Moman and Dan Penn once wrote a song that Aretha Franklin recorded and immortalized called "Do Right Woman, Do Right Man," that asserted "If you want a do right all day woman, you got to be a do right all night man." (It sounds *way* cooler when she says it.) Bad behavior on the part of either spouse never justifies reciprocation. That being said, when we, as men, do the right things, our wives will find it much easier to keep the Lord's commands to them, especially when it comes to honoring their husbands.

So what has the Lord commanded us to do as husbands? In Genesis 2:24, God explains that for marriage "a man shall leave his father and mother and be joined to his wife, and they shall become one flesh" (NKJV). One teaching from this verse is that when a man marries, he and his wife, and nobody else, become one flesh. The man is the one who is directed by God to leave his father and mother (Gen. 2:24). He leaves to establish his own home for himself and his wife. They alone will lay down together at night, live with their decisions, and deal with the consequences. For that reason, they must go out on their own and seek the Lord's guidance for themselves. That is not to say that they should never listen to the wisdom of their parents anymore. But they must realize that only they can make the decision whether or not to allow God to build their home.

Proverbs 5:18 teaches us that a husband should "rejoice in the wife of [his] youth" (ESV). And verse 19 closes by telling a husband to "always be enraptured with her love" (NKJV). What commandment could possibly be more enjoyable than that? I should always love my wife and always be in awe of her and her love for me. Does your wife know that you love her? How do you let her know? Does she know that you are amazed by her and her love for you? Again, how do you let her know? Now, no one else can tell you what to do or how to do it. Everyone is different and every relationship is different. That's for you and her to find out together, so get after it and savor every moment.

Ephesians 5:25 instructs husbands to "love your wives, just as Christ also loved the church and gave Himself up for her" (NASB). Do you give yourself up for your wife? Does the way that you work say that you give yourself up for her? Does what you do after work say that you give yourself up for her?

What this all boils down to is that if we will keep God's commands concerning our treatment of our wives, then our wives will find it much easier to keep his commands to them. It just makes sense.

Family Heritage

Every family has a heritage. We have all inherited a name that carries meaning with those who know it. Some people inherit names that they have to live down. Some spend their lives trying to live up to theirs. Some seek to uphold theirs and continue the good they have seen in their families. My great-grandfather (the husband of 100/100) was a child of an abusive alcoholic. Statistics suggest that abused children and children of alcoholics are likely to display the same tendencies as adults; however, my great-grandfather (we call him "Daddy Bob") trusted the Lord and set a different course for his life and for his family. Because God saved one man, my children, four generations after him, have inherited a better name.

What name were you born into? If your family heritage needs to change, then let the Lord start with you. We are not doomed to become the weaknesses of our parents. Romans

6:8–10 says: "Now if we have died with Christ, we believe that we shall also live with Him, knowing that Christ, having been raised from the dead, is never to die again; death no longer is master over him. For the death that He died, He died to sin once for all; but the life that he lives, He lives to God" (NASB). We follow in his footsteps, walking no longer under the mastery of death, whatever form it may take, but instead in obedience to his Holy Spirit.

CHAPTER 4

Get it Done, Have Fun, and Let them Help

One of fatherhood's easiest responsibilities to carry out is also one of its easiest to mess up. We need to do the things we do with our kids, and we need to do it the right way.

Most people know that men have responsibilities to accomplish. Often those responsibilities manifest themselves in the form of a list. That list is often not in our handwriting. Don't misunderstand this list. Some men see the list and think something like, "Well, now I can't go fishing today." Others see the list and think something like, "Well, now she's going to be mad when I get home from fishing today." A great man, however, remembers that the list is a request for a labor of love from a woman to her one man, to do the things that she needs done. It's the woman he loves, doing what he used to only dream about, namely, coming to him when there's something to do that she can't do without him. Don't whine and shrink back, especially not in front of the kids. Have some respect for yourself. Put on those jeans. (You know the ones I'm talking about. If you actually don't know what I'm talking about, then I apologize for how weird it must be to read this right now.) Get your work gloves out. I like to put them in my back pocket with the fingers sticking out a little. And, if it gets serious, I put them on. If you have sons, suit them up too. They'll love it, and so will you. If your daughters want in, let them in. It's very important to teach our boys to get things done with the right attitude. It can literally change lives.

Baseball, Household Chores, and how the Residual Cultural Effects of Designing Women Influenced the Outcome of the 2000 Presidential Election

Tragically, fatherhood is a field where just showing up puts us in the top half, but we have to remember that we're not graded on a curve. Our children must know that we want to be with them, just as the Lord wants to be with his children.

For some parents, absenteeism is not a problem. But many parents (especially fathers) make the mistake of forcing their children into the activities that they enjoyed or were good at. Many times these vicarious obsessions tend to push children away and cause all kinds of problems, not the least of which is a sense that they are not loved unconditionally.

My parents loved seeing us do the things that made us happy. My sister, my brother, and I all took up a variety of activities, and our parents took an interest and supported us in all of them. One of mine was running. I mention this one because my parents' support of my running demonstrated the lengths that they went to for me, like few other things can. My parents traveled all over southeast Texas in all kinds of weather to see me run. For some track meets, they would drive more than an hour just to sit in the stands for a few more hours to see me run for sometimes as little as two minutes.

Now that I'm a parent myself, I understand better why they did what they did for us. I love to see my kids doing the things that they love. And the beautiful thing is that by encouraging them in the things that they want to do, or at least try out, they are more willing to join me in the things that I like to do.

My daddy was a baseball player when he was growing up. All three of his kids tried our hands at baseball or softball. I was the least talented of all of us and had a short career before moving on to other activities, but I still love baseball like few other people I know. That love has come from a history of playing, watching, and talking baseball with my daddy and my brother, as well as some close friends. For me it has always been something that we could do together, one way or another. These kinds of activities are important for us to share with our children, as they provide us with an opportunity to communicate and get to know each other.

I intend to have the same relationship with each of my kids. It may or may not be baseball for us. It may be something different with each of my kids. That's okay. The experience with each other leads to a better knowledge of and trust in each other. And just like Romans 10:17 teaches, "faith comes by hearing, and hearing by the word of God" (NKJV), so does our children's ability to trust us comes from experience with us.

I also remember doing some household chores with my daddy. I remember him teaching me to mow and weed-eat, thereby teaching me to take care of nice tools that make work easier and preparing me to take care of a home. I remember riding around with my daddy running errands. Those times allowed us to talk. We listened to all kinds of music. Many of my musical tastes were formed in those years. I'm grateful now that while many of my peers were being shaped by MTV, videogames, and Metallica, I was with people who loved me.

No matter how anti-family our culture may become, we

must continue to be daddies to our children. We need to be the ones to teach them about life, work, love, the opposite sex, right and wrong, sideburns, etc. Our enemy, the devil, wants badly to break down our families. Don't give your family over to any substitutes.

Whatever you may be doing, let your kids in. Let them ride when you have to run to town. It doesn't have to be anything special. Just doing things together makes it special.

While doing things with our kids, whether it be working, playing, or just being together, it is important to do it right. Daddies have the power to make any activity awesome for their kids, but we also have the power to suck the fun out of any activity for them, too. I'm not proud of this, but I can make that statement with confidence because I have done both.

What it all boils down to is to love them like nobody else can. They only get one daddy. We only get one shot at being daddy for each child. There are some things that nobody else can do like we can. There are some things that they don't want to do and some moments that they don't want to have with anyone else. There is a safety in experiencing everything that life brings with daddy. The knowledge that he'll be there changes everything. No moment is trivial or meaningless with your daddy.

CHAPTER 5

Name

A MAN'S NAME IS of the utmost importance. A name carries a reputation. We start out with names that we did nothing to earn. Some people start out with bad names through no fault of their own. Others start out with good names that they did nothing to earn. These names usually come with high expectations. Still others start out in new places where their names are clean slates, and it is up to them to make something of them; however, we can be sure that we will make names for ourselves, whether we want to or not.

Our names can make life difficult for us. They can open doors for us. As if that's not sobering enough, they can also make things difficult for our children. A woman who marries leaves the name that she has always known and been known by, and takes the name of her husband, a tremendous show of faith that often goes overlooked (not unlike the decision to cast the great John Wayne as Genghis Khan in *The Conqueror*).

The Lord teaches us about our names by the things that he says about his own name. Now, I don't mean to equate God's name with our names in any way; however, he demonstrates that names (his and ours) are very important to him, and what is important to the Lord should be important to us.

He teaches us in Proverbs 22:1 "A good name is to be more desired than great riches, favor is better than silver and gold" (NASB). It is of the utmost importance that our word be good. Our wives, kids, and the other people in our lives need to know that we do what we say we will do. If we do not deliver on our word, then the people whom we deal with will come to expect us to be unreliable. Coming back from a bad reputation, once it has been established, is very difficult.

If our kids cannot rely upon us to keep our word, then they will learn quickly that none of the words of their daddies mean anything, commitments or otherwise. Once our word is sacrificed, we compromise the standing to discipline, teach, and provide emotional stability to our children. It has often been said that a child's father shapes the way that the child views God; therefore, a father whose word is meaningless has the potential to cause a tremendous amount of damage to his children and their ability to trust the Lord.

Our timeless example, Jesus, took upon his name the gravest single responsibility in history, upon which every human life relies. Luke 24:47 records Jesus' own words, saying, "repentance for forgiveness of sins should be proclaimed in His name to all the nations" (ESV). For the sake of our salvation, Jesus' name had to be trustworthy. For that reason, David writes in Psalm 138:2, "You have magnified Your word above all Your name" (NKJV).

In the same way, each of us must acknowledge the relationship between his name and his word. Our families, co-workers, and everyone else around us are right to expect us to be men of our word. The world around us says that a man ought to do and say whatever he has to. To such men I say (in love): grow up. Stop breaking the hearts of the people who love you. Instead, give them nothing less than a glimpse of the character of God.

Once, when I was in college, I found myself with conflicting commitments. To be honest, I had a problem with double-booking in those days, but this particular instance was especially memorable. My great-grandfather had been a "sawmiller," and in his retirement, he made bed slats and sold them to some of his old clients. Once age made deliveries difficult, he began to ask me to make the shipment runs, which I was happy to make. On this occasion, I had slipped up once again and made another commitment on the same day.

When talking with daddy about it, he said, "If your word ain't no good, you ain't no good." I felt ashamed as I understood the importance of my word, something I had always verbally acknowledged, but now felt its weight. My word, which I had handled so flippantly, had meant more to the other men in my family than it had to me. It was a humbling thing to see a name that the men in my family had worked hard to establish as one of faithfulness and honesty, being handed off to me.

It was not an easy lesson, but it was a necessary one. Our world is starving to death for this lesson, but many are not willing to teach it. Gentlemen, it's our job.

CHAPTER 6

Fighting Evil

WE LIVE IN a world that demands that we not recognize good and evil, which raises the question: "Who wouldn't want me to recognize evil when I see it?" This is not a trick question. Of course, someone who is about the business of evil would not want me to recognize what he is up to. The philosophies of subjectivism, relativism, and postmodernism are inherently evil. Don't take my word for it. Look around you. If you can find one example of anything good that has ever come from these philosophies, then feel free to return the unused portion of this publication, no hard feelings.

Evil is a destructive force. It seeks to enslave and harm whomever it may. Man is, by nature, evil (Matt. 7:11). This is not an opinion or an academic theory. It is the Word of God and is self-evident. When we repent of evil and entrust ourselves to the salvation provided by the Lord, he makes us righteous, and calls us to live according to his Holy Spirit instead of the flesh, or our evil nature.

Now, as former slaves to evil, our enemy is not our fellow man who still lives according to evil. Instead, our enemy is the devil, who exerts his influence in this world in an attempt to destroy as many of us as he can. His objective in hurting people is to ultimately hurt God, who loves people. As we live in this world, we are called by the Lord to carry the truth to those who are enslaved, as we once were, and to combat evil in their hearts, so that they may hear, believe, and be saved. So, under the direction of the Holy Spirit, we are God's warriors in this world, fighting evil and rescuing the people of the world, whom the Lord loves so much that he gave his life for them.

We must not succumb to the postmodern idea that good and evil do not exist, or that they are nothing more than "oppressive social constructs." Good and evil do exist, as defined by God. Not only do they exist, but they are also intuitive to a high degree. Whether we will be honest about it or not, we know that dishonesty is wrong; we know that murder is wrong; we know that adultery is wrong; we know that stealing is wrong. The Lord has even said that we all know that he is God (Rom. 1:18–20). Many who would deny this truth perform some impressive intellectual gymnastics to arrive at their positions. If you want proof, watch how quickly they will speak up when someone wrongs them.

This is one reason that Christians must take God at his Word, as well as letting the evidence speak for itself, and understand that he created the world and everything in it exactly and literally as he outlined in the Bible. If we accept Darwinian evolution, as many "Christians" do, then we accept the premise that we are nothing more than chemicals that, through happenstance, developed a drive to insure the proliferation of our genetics. To believe that lie is to believe that no law exists except to survive and reproduce. The consequences of this thinking are evident all around us in the form of (you guessed it) evil. And where relativist, postmodern thinking prevails, evil goes unchecked.

We do not have the authority to define right and wrong; the

Lord has established that already. Our job is to acknowledge God by correctly identifying right and wrong. Our job is to stand firm on the Word of the Lord and hold lawlessness back. This may only be done by the Holy Spirit (2 Thess. 2:7), who lives and works in those who have entrusted their lives to God through Jesus.

David

One of the all-time great heroes of fighting evil has to be David for several reasons. First Samuel 17 provides us with an awesome and familiar reason for a real man to fight evil. The account includes some very important intricacies that should not go overlooked.

First Samuel 17:1 tells us that the Philistines had gathered their armies for battle at Sochoh in Ephes Dammim, which belongs to Judah. Evil had encroached upon the land that belonged to the tribe of Judah, to which young David belonged. Throughout history, evil has followed a pattern of testing men's responses when it advances beyond its boundaries. All tyrants and oppressors test the waters before making power grabs. These tests allow the perpetrators to gauge to what extent they will be allowed to proceed with their plans.

Not if, but when evil comes to see if we or our homes and families may be taken, we have to respond like David did. He knew that the Lord had already spoken for the land that belonged to his tribe. David looked around him and saw no fence post to keep evil behind the boundary that the Lord had established. Even the name Ephes Dammim, where David and Goliath took their stands, means "boundary of blood-drops." We need to understand that keeping evil from our homes will be a fight. The boundary of blood-drops must be defended. So, young David said to King Saul, the man who should have stood against Goliath, "Let no man's heart fail because of him; your servant will go and fight with this Philistine" (1 Sam. 17:32 NKJV).

King Saul protested, but David's matter of fact answer was the response of a man who had lived his life trusting the Lord. In First Samuel 17:34–36 David said,

> Your servant used to keep his father's sheep, and when a lion or a bear came and took a lamb out of the flock, I went out after it and struck it, and delivered the lamb from its mouth; and when it arose against me, I caught it by its beard, and struck and killed it. Your servant has killed both lion and bear; and this uncircumcised Philistine will be like one of them, seeing he has defied the armies of the living God. (NKJV)

David understood that evil had crossed its boundary, and that it would only continue to do so if left unchecked. David had spent his life guarding the flock and regularly killed wild beasts that, by all reasoning, should have killed him. David's life was always in the hands of the Lord. So is everyone else's, but the difference is that David acknowledged it and lived by it. David knew that the one God had been provoked, and his name had been blasphemed. All he had to do was line up with the Lord, which was easy for him because he was already there.

Later, David added "The Lord who delivered me from the paw of the lion and from the paw of the bear, he will deliver me from the hand of this Philistine" (1 Sam. 17:37 NASB). Because of David's history with God, he knew that he could trust the Lord.

Do you have a history with God? Has your life been a story of the faithfulness of the Lord? If the answer is no, then get started today. Take him at his Word. Without the precedent of having lived in close relationship with God, it is very difficult to stand as David did and confront evil when it comes for your home.

Evil is like grass. We can't just mow it once; it will come back as long as it goes unchecked. Evil will cross the boundary. We didn't go looking for the fight. It would be nice if the fight would be won by polite discourse, but after all, it is called "the boundary of blood-drops" for a reason. The fight is coming whether we want it or not. We have to fight because if we don't, no one else will.

Hezekiah

One of the many great historical accounts detailed in the Bible is the record of the Assyrian threat against Jerusalem in the eighth century B. C. Just like Goliath and the Philistines crossing over into land that God had given to his people, this time the Assyrians laid claim by right of military might to the city that the Lord calls his own (Ps. 46:4). As always, you would do well to read the biblical account yourself in Second Kings 18–19, Second Chronicles 32, and Isaiah 36–37. Every man needs to be ready for the fight against evil, and this particular confrontation provides us with a wealth of wisdom with which to equip ourselves.

We learn in Second Kings 16 and the beginning of chapter 18 that Hezekiah's father, King Ahaz, had left the kingdom in poor shape for his son. Ahaz "did not do what was right in the sight of the Lord his God" (2 Kings 16:2 NASB), but instead engaged in the worship of other gods, even to the point of child sacrifice. But chapter 18 teaches us that Hezekiah cleaned house when he began to rule in Judah. Hezekiah led the nation to return to the Lord and to serve him alone. But, he learned one lesson very quickly when the Assyrian army threatened Jerusalem.

Trial by Fire

Like Hezekiah found out, evil loves to test its limits when there is a changing of the guard. As soon as Hezekiah turned the kingdom back to the Lord, his resolve to honor God was tried. We should expect the same. We have to make up our minds where we stand and bring our families up to know those boundaries. And, if we want them to stand, our boundaries must be God's boundaries.

At this time in history, the Assyrian army was a formidable power. They went wherever they pleased and got what they wanted. When the Assyrian king, Sennacherib, threatened Jerusalem, he included in his letter a list of other kingdoms that he had taken and whose gods had not been able to deliver them from his hand (2 Kings 18:34–35). He even posed the question to the men of the city: would Jerusalem's God be able to save his city?

Here we have the same formula that was in place in First Samuel 17. Evil set itself up as God. The same story plays out in our lives. In a million different ways, evil seeks to come into our homes, to have our families, and to discredit the one God in our minds and in the minds of our children. When Hezekiah prayed in Second Kings 19:17–18, he acknowledged that the Assyrian king had, in fact, taken other kingdoms, but that he had done so because the gods of those kingdoms "were not gods but the work of men's hands" (2 Kings 19:18 NASB). In the same way, we should understand that even though others around us may compromise the Word of God and subsequently falter and fall, in the day of trouble the child of God will be able to stand (Eph. 6:13).

In Second Kings 18:19, the first words out of the mouth of the servant of Sennacherib were, "What confidence is this in which you trust?" (NKJV). When we are second-guessed, what will our response be? Will we just lie down and chalk it up to changing times? Remember, the Lord, his Word, and his men are timeless. Will we be too afraid to teach our children to live by God's Word rather than the demands of this world because we don't think that we can live up to that standard? That's the very reason that the Lord has told us not to place our confidence in the flesh (Phil. 3:3).

So, to answer the Assyrian king's question, our confidence is the name of the Lord our God (Ps. 20:7). The Assyrian king and whoever else defies the one God would do well to consider what confidence they trust in.

In verse 25, the threats take a different form. The messenger says, "Have I now come up without the Lord against this place to destroy it? The Lord said to me, 'Go up against this land, and destroy it'" (2 Kings 18:25 NKJV). When faced with what appears to be a no-win situation, we easily begin to think that God has abandoned us or even turned against us.

In times like these, I remember nautical twilight. The U. S. Naval Observatory defines nautical twilight as the time when the center of the sun is 12 degrees below the horizon. Given the sun's position, during nautical twilight, very little is visible, making navigation, or anything else for that matter, difficult; however, the horizon is visible as well as some brighter stars, making it the perfect opportunity to take readings by the stars with the horizon as a reference. Nautical twilight is a short window of time, during which navigation by sight is difficult and dangerous, but the constancy of the horizon and the stars provide truth by which we can navigate.

I believe that nautical twilight is one of many signs that God has built into his world to direct us to him. His Word is truth.

Truth is immovable no matter how hard we may try to change that. We have to align ourselves with the truth or spend our lives in frustration and denial. Psalm 32:6 admonishes "everyone who is godly" to pray to the Lord "in a time when You may be found" (NKJV). Psalm 69:13 also follows this theme, saying "But as for me, my prayer is to You, O Lord, in the acceptable time; O God, in the multitude of Your mercy, hear me in the truth of Your salvation" (NKJV).

Like Hezekiah, sometimes we find ourselves in situations that don't look like we thought they would. The Assyrian messenger lied and said that they had been sent by God to conquer Jerusalem. Now, an army that, by all appearances, was unstoppable confronted Hezekiah—in spite of the king's faithful service to the Lord. In times like those, the man of God must stand on the Word of God. And, as the verses from Psalms direct, we have to prepare for those times by seeking the Lord beforehand, "in a time of finding out," in that time of nautical twilight. If we will allow him to make us ready, then when the darkness comes and things do not look like they should, we will know the truth and will be able to live by faith and not by sight.

Undermining the Truth

Another tactic that evil will employ to try to discourage God's people is depicted in Second Kings 18:26–30. Here, King Hezekiah's messengers asked the Assyrian messenger to speak with them in his native language so that others would not understand and lose heart when they heard the threats. In response, the messenger "called out with a loud voice in Hebrew," and declared: "Do not let Hezekiah deceive you, for he shall not be able to deliver you... nor let Hezekiah make you trust in the Lord" (NKJV).

Our enemy, the devil, is a ruthless enemy. He will try to frighten our children and persuade them not to trust the Lord. He will try to make it appear as though we, their parents, are going down with a sinking ship. We already see an effort on the part of our depraved culture to convince our children that we have deceived them and that everyone will inevitably come around to their way of thinking.

Our children must see us living as Hezekiah lived. Just as he turned Judah away from the worship of other gods, and restored the kingdom to God alone, we must also build our homes on the Word of the Lord. And, when the threats arise we have to continue to stand on God's Word, just like we did when things were easier. We can't afford to wait until trouble comes to get our houses in order.

Verses 31–33 may be the most telling of the entire threatening message. In those verses, the messenger of doom says, "Make peace with me by a present and come out to me; and every one of you eat from his own vine and every one from his own fig tree, and every one of you drink the waters of his own cistern; until I come and take you away to a land like your own land" (2 Kings 18:31–32 NKJV). The Assyrian offer was the height of condescension, and make no mistake, this world makes us the same offer. If we will only recant our confession of faith in the one God and his Son Jesus, we will be taken care of. If we will only play by the rules of a rebellious culture, we will be left alone.

This verse brings to mind Ronald Reagan's iconic "A Time for Choosing" speech wherein he famously declared, "there's only one guaranteed way you can have peace—and you can have it in the next second—surrender."[12] Gentlemen, we must never surrender our families over to the enemy who desires their destruction. They have been bought with the blood of Jesus, and we must not dare to profane that sacrifice by breaking faith with him and abandoning our children to be assimilated into depravity.

Notice also that the Assyrian king promises to take them to a land "like" their own (2 Kings 18:32 NKJV). What has been given to us by God himself is irreplaceable. The Assyrian king had the arrogance to approach the city that had been promised to the Hebrew people, to claim it as his own, and to demand that they become his subjects, pay him tribute, and be relocated to a land "like" their own. In the same way, our heritage from the Lord was given by him alone and will not be taken from us, even in death. For, we know whom we have believed and are convinced that he is able to guard what we have entrusted to him until that day (2 Tim. 1:12).

The Assyrian offer has been the offer of tyrants, dictators, and usurpers of authority throughout history. "I will take care of you, if you will only hand over your freedom to me." They speak these lies to people whom they have deceived into believing that they are downtrodden and oppressed by someone else (in this case, Hezekiah and, ultimately, God). Sennacherib wanted to convince the people of Jerusalem that God was needlessly putting them in harm's way. If King Hezekiah had seen himself as a victim here, he may have excused himself from trusting the Lord. He could have used the circumstances as justification for surrender, but that's not what God's people should do.

Why Should we Expect to Stand When Others Fall?

The next psychological battering ram that the Assyrian messenger goes to in his effort to bring down the faith of God's people is history. On two occasions, Hezekiah is reminded of the other kings who tried to resist the Assyrian army and fell (2 Kings 18:33–35; 19:11–13). The Assyrian king even asks: "Has any of the gods of the nations at all delivered its land from the hand of the king of Assyria?" (2 Kings 18:33 NKJV).

In the same way, we can look around us and see other men who have fallen. We can see other families who have fallen prey to all kinds of temptations. But, that's not all we can see. The Lord sets before us in Hebrews chapters 11 and 12 "so great a cloud of witnesses surrounding us" (12:1 NASB), saints who stood because they lived by faith in the Word of God. Then in Hebrews 13:7, we are urged to "Remember those who led [us], who spoke the word of God to [us]," and we are instructed to consider "the result of their conduct," and "imitate their faith" (NASB).

Hezekiah saw through the list of fallen kingdoms that were crushed under the feet of Assyria. When Hezekiah prayed in Second Kings 19:17–18, he acknowledged before the Lord that "the kings of Assyria have devastated the nations and their lands and have cast their gods into the fire, for they were not gods but the work of men's hands, wood and stone. So they have destroyed them" (NASB). When we see the fallen around us, we need to understand where their allegiances lie before we begin to fret that the same fate will overtake us. Instead, we need to understand that the Lord has never abandoned those whose hearts are set on him.

As was discussed earlier, when Hezekiah received the threatening message, he responded in a way that is nothing less than beautiful. The child of God "received the letter from the hand of the messengers, and read it; and Hezekiah went up to the house of the Lord, and spread it before the Lord" (2 Kings 19:14 NKJV). Think about that imagery for a minute. Whether he knew it or not, Hezekiah set an example of humility and perfect faith. Whatever evils threaten our families or us must be taken and spread out before the Almighty God. The prayers of his children are precious to him (2 Sam. 22; Ps. 18; Rev. 5:8).

So, how does Hezekiah teach us to fight evil? We fight evil by standing before the enemy and kneeling before the Lord. When we know what God himself has said, the lies of the enemy are shown for what they are.

Josiah

King Josiah is another man we can look at in the Bible who fought evil in a situation that was similar to Hezekiah's, with a few important differences. Both inherited the throne of Judah from their fathers who had done evil. Both of their fathers had led the kingdom into sin and left a culture of depravity for their sons to rule. One important difference, though, is that Hezekiah was twenty-five years old when he began to reign, whereas Josiah was only eight.

The first act of Josiah that is recorded in the Bible was his order for the temple of the Lord to be repaired (2 Kings 22:3–7). As the king, Josiah could have done whatever he wanted. Certainly, no moral precedents set by his father would have led him to honor God, but this young man chose to rebuild the temple of the Lord.

As a high school teacher, I often hear teenagers saying things like, "We're kids; we're supposed to [fill in the blank with the self-destructive activity of your choice]." Other times they assert, "I'll get my life together when I'm older." And, of course, "Mr. Chumley, has anyone ever told you that you bear a striking resemblance to Matthew McConaughey, Shaun Cassidy, *and* Denzel Washington, if only they had been better-looking?" It is a lie of our enemy, the devil, that in our youth we are excused from acknowledging God. Josiah stepped out from a culture that expected him to behave like his father had, and instead, he set about repairing the temple.

Josiah repairing the temple is much like the time when Elijah faced an entire nation that had turned its back on God (1 Kings 18:30). Once the prophets of Baal had cried out to their god and even injured and humiliated themselves to no avail, Elijah called the people to him and "repaired the altar of the Lord that was broken down" (1 Kings 18:30 NKJV). Keep reading if you don't know the rest of the story, but I want to focus on that one act. In both men's cultures, God had been forsaken. His places of worship were in ruins.

Both men separated themselves from what was accepted as "normal," and honored the one Lord of all other gods. At eighteen years old, Josiah rejected the lie that he was too young to be held accountable for whether or not he did what was right. The idea that youth should be a time of irresponsibility is not harmless, cute, or acceptable. It's evil. And it has claimed countless lives. Like Josiah, we have to reject this thinking without qualification.

In Second Kings 22, we see the young king apprised of the finding of the book of the law. When he heard the Word of God, Josiah tore his clothes in repentance (2 Kings 22:11). Josiah then took the Word of the Lord and "he read in their hearing all the words of the Book of the Covenant" (23:2 NKJV).

Let's take a moment to recognize an awesome moment in history. King Josiah was putting Romans 10 into practice about 700 years before it was written! "How then will they call on Him in whom they have not believed? How will they believe in Him whom they have not heard? And how will they hear without a preacher? . . . So faith comes from hearing, and hearing by the word of Christ" (Rom. 10:14, 17 NASB).

We need to understand from this parallel that we should "remember those who led [us], who spoke the word of God to [us]; and considering the result of their conduct, imitate their faith. Jesus Christ is the same yesterday and today and forever" (Heb. 13:7–8 NASB). Today, we can and should follow in Josiah's steps and preach the Word of God, so that those around us can put their faith in him.

Josiah fought evil by confronting it with the truth. Many people in our lives need to come into contact with the Word of the Lord. If we rely on someone else to bring God's Word, then we not only exclude ourselves from a work that he has for us, but we also withhold life-saving truth from people who are so precious to the Lord that he did not even spare his own life to offer them redemption.

God has told us that in these last days, that the world will plunge deeper into rebellion against him (2 Tim. 3). But one of his purposes for us, the saints, is to offer his grace to those who have not yet trusted him. Because he does not wish "for any to perish but for all to come to repentance" (2 Pet. 3:9 NASB), we should want the same thing. And the way we fight the evil deception that ensnares so many is by doing exactly what Josiah did. We shine the light on it, and we bring the Word of the Lord to them. Even though the world will continue to deteriorate, lives can still be saved and families can still be restored; hope remains for anyone who will call on the name of the Lord.

Caleb

Caleb is best known for standing alongside Joshua on the promise of God against the entire nation of Israel. The Lord had promised to give Canaan to the Israelites, but no one among them believed the promise except for Joshua and Caleb. As a result, Joshua and Caleb received a confirmation from God that he would see to it that they lived to take Canaan, even after all those who rebelled against him had fallen in the wilderness.

Forty years later, my favorite episode featuring Caleb took place. In this story, eighty-five-year-old Caleb approached

Joshua for his blessing as he went to take the land that the Lord had given him (Josh. 14:6–12).

The land that God had promised to Caleb was the "hill country." The Anakim lived in the hill country. Based on Deuteronomy 1:28, 2:10, and 9:2, we know that the Anakim were giants. In the same way, "giants" want to occupy our homes today. They take many forms, but they can all be reduced down to evil. They all want to see just how much we will tolerate. Some of the common giants we face are: dishonesty, hypocrisy, unbelief, unfaithfulness, sexual immorality of all kinds, disobedience, disregard for the Word of God, and unwholesome talk. Our enemy, the devil, must shriek with laughter every time a Christian home opens its doors to the lusts that are so prevalent in our dying culture.

We must defend our homes against evil. Our families need their homes to be safe places where they can know that they will not have to continue the fight that rages outside our doors. I still remember an incident from my childhood when a snake made its way into our house. My daddy killed it. I don't understand why more daddies aren't willing to do the same. In fact, far too many invite death into their homes.

Evil will always be eager to test our boundaries. Evil does not leave voluntarily. If you let it go unchecked, you'll come home from work to find it in your recliner with a sandwich, watching a game that you really don't care about, yelling at the television with its mouth full. And then you'll find its socks in weird places around the house for the next few days. You'll eventually find yourself sitting at the kitchen table in the middle of the night, wringing your hands, wondering where the kids learned to say those things. So many fathers look up one day and ask, "How did we get here?" The tragic answer is in the mirror.

Like us, Caleb had been given a home, but it had to be taken.

Our homes must be established, guarded, and from time-to-time, fought for. When we are newly married, everything that we do establishes a precedent for how we will make decisions, how we will spend our time, and what kind of homes we will have. Too many times, the wrong precedents are established. Money becomes the driver for many of our decisions; our children become afterthoughts; honoring the Word of the Lord falls by the wayside. We allow these evils, thinking something like, "It's just too hard; surely God understands."

We need to understand, like Caleb did, that our homes have been given to us. Even though the world around us will continue to deteriorate, the Lord has told us how to build our homes and raise our families. God gave Caleb the victory, and he gives us the victory if we are willing to trust him and fight the fight. The Lord does not intend his men to live defeated, watching helplessly while their families are enticed away and succumb to evil. Instead, he told us to teach his Word diligently to our children and to "not provoke [our] children to anger; but bring them up in the discipline and instruction of the Lord" (Eph. 6:4 NASB).

I love how the historical record of Caleb's possession of the hill country moves from Joshua 14:13, where Joshua blesses Caleb, to verse 14, "therefore, Hebron became the inheritance of Caleb" (NASB). Once Caleb had trusted God's Word, the battle was a formality, a foregone conclusion.

The world is dying for more men to stand as Caleb did, men who will run evil out of their homes. Tolerance of evil in our homes is a game that we can't afford to play with our children's lives. When was the last time that your kids were reassured that their daddy guards their home against the evil that rages outside? When was the last time that they knew that comfort? If the answer is not flattering, then today is a good time to make it right.

Elijah

One of my all-time favorite fighters of evil is Elijah (cue southern rock theme music over a montage of various scenes including the mocking of the prophets of Baal, the widow's son rising up from his deathbed, Elijah standing before King Ahab speaking the Word of God, and Ahab grimacing while rubbing his temples and guzzling Maalox).

Elijah lived during the reign of one of Israel's most infamous kings, and that's saying something, considering the field. King Ahab actively led the nation of Israel away from God. In First Kings 16:30–33 we can see that Ahab "did evil in the sight of the Lord more than all who were before him" (1 Kings 16:30 NASB). He even behaved as though "it had been a trivial thing for him to walk in the sins of Jeroboam" (1 Kings 16:31 NKJV), the first king of Israel once it split from Judah. Ahab led the nation to worship other gods and even built a house for the god Baal, with an altar, in addition to setting up the Asherah, another idol. "Ahab did more to provoke the Lord God of Israel to anger than all the kings of Israel who were before him" (1 Kings 16:33b NKJV).

Elijah lived in an era when evil advanced quickly and met with little resistance. These times should sound very familiar to us; however, there was resistance from one man (cue southern rock theme music—okay, I'll stop for now). In his day, Elijah fought evil by shining the light on it. He spoke the Word of the Lord to the king himself, and he was able to do so because he knew something. In First Kings 17:1, Elijah made his first recorded appearance by proclaiming God's judgment to Ahab; Elijah said, "As the Lord, the God of Israel lives, before whom I stand, there shall not be dew nor rain these years, except at my word" (NKJV).

One important point that we need to pay attention to is

that Elijah said "before whom I stand" (1 Kings 17:1 NKJV), speaking of the Lord. He did not speak his own word or in his own authority, but instead he spoke God's Word by the authority of the Lord. Likewise, as we stand against evil in our day, we will fail if we speak our words in our authority, as so many do. But, if we speak the timeless Word of the Lord that accomplishes its purpose (Isa. 55:10–11), then we will not speak in vain.

James 5:17 reminds us that "Elijah was a man with a nature like ours, and he prayed earnestly that it would not rain, and it did not rain on the earth for three years and six months" (NASB). God wants us to understand that Elijah was not a special case, but that Elijah was human like us. The Lord intends that his people should speak his Word, showing evil for what it is in the world today. In doing so, we will warn those who are headed for danger.

The account of Elijah on Mt. Carmel is the scene where he confronted evil in Israel and exposed it for what it was, and in this act, Elijah arms us with important tactics that we can use when confronting evil (1 Kings 18).

First, Elijah took the truth before the people. In our world today, we can see that several blatantly false beliefs are widely accepted as truth. Among them are: Darwinian evolution, the supposed merits of communism/socialism, and Madonna's talent. Our culture has largely accepted lies like these as truth without a shred of credible evidence. In times like these, it is incumbent upon those who know the truth (not that we are in any way better, but because we stopped denying what has been made plain to us according to Romans 1:18–32) to take the truth out into the world. The darkness of evil and deception go unchecked where the light of truth is absent. The Scriptures teach that deceit is the devil's only "real" weapon (Gen. 3:5; 2 Cor. 11:14; 2 John 7; Rev. 18:23), and we must heed that warning.

Second, with the attention of the people of Israel, Elijah called out their indecision. The Israelites wanted to serve both God and Baal, you know, just in case God didn't come through for them. But Elijah knew that the Lord will have no rivals in the hearts of his people. Elijah was confronting an evil that is prevalent today, the philosophy of universalism. It is questionable whether or not the proponents of universalism actually believe what they profess, since its most fundamental tenet is self-contradictory. Universalism, in its most liberal forms, equates all systems of belief as equally valid, and ultimately leading to a supreme deity. This belief cannot be true, as most (if not all) religions are mutually exclusive.

The possibility exists that most adherents to universalism choose to accept its teachings out of convenience, as it excuses us from acknowledgement of the existence of truth. As was the case in Israel, our world needs us to call these beliefs what they are: lies. Regardless of how it makes us feel, our decisions carry consequences. In the name of compassion, we are taught that we must honor all beliefs as valid (with the noteworthy exception of biblical truth).

As the Lord's men who understand that Jesus laid down his life as the only acceptable sacrifice for our sin, we must love people enough to tell the truth. Our enemy, the devil, takes people captive under "the rulers . . . the powers . . . the world forces of this darkness... [and] the spiritual forces of wickedness in the heavenly places" (Eph. 6:12 NASB). Tolerance will turn a blind eye to the poison, and affirm the victim, thinking that he is doing him a favor. Love will bring into the light the things that are dark and will not withhold the only one who can save. In the footsteps of Elijah, our responsibility as men is to set the choice before our world every day, in the name of love.

Finally, Elijah reminded the Israelites of the actions of their forefathers who had served the Lord faithfully when "he repaired the altar of the Lord that was broken down" (1 Kings

18:30 NKJV). Like Elijah, we can approach the "torn down altars" where we live.

The popular philosophy of progressivism would have us reject old ways for no other reason than that they are old. (Never mind that the average progressive swears by some of the oldest and most devastatingly destructive ideas in history.) Some things do change. Truth is not one of them. Natural law and a reasonably objective observation of history lead to the conclusion that when man departs from truth, the results are catastrophic. A few examples include (but are not limited to): Marxism (again), the French and Russian revolutions, and the 1976 Chicago White Sox uniforms.

Following Elijah's example, we must restore God's timeless Word to its rightful place in our hearts and in our homes. Hebrews 13:7 urges us to "Remember those who led you, who spoke the word of God to you; and considering the result of their conduct, imitate their faith" (NASB).

Mt. Carmel was not the only place where Elijah called on men to remember and consider the faithfulness of their forefathers. Later, Elijah wrote a letter to King Jehoram of Judah, warning him of God's coming judgment because he had not "walked in the ways of Jehoshaphat [his] father, or in the ways of Asa king of Judah" (2 Chron. 21:12 NKJV). Men should always consider what others have done, good or bad, and heed the warnings as well as the encouragements that their ways of life demonstrate.

Read the rest of the account if you're not familiar with it (or if you are). On Mt. Carmel, both Baal and God were called upon to burn their respective offerings. Only one answered. Now, the decision whether or not to follow the Lord faithfully was still in the hands of each individual. But Elijah had obeyed God and showed the lies for what they were, and so can we.

Jeremiah

If we intend to stand against evil, we need to know that we will face resistance. A depraved world will not welcome the light that shows it for what it is. But, as we will see with Jeremiah's story, even when it seems like no one wants to listen, God's Word still accomplishes his purpose. Thank you, Lord!

Jeremiah understood what it was like to be God's prophet working during a time of crisis. He had spoken the Word of the Lord to the people of Judah, and in return Pashhur the priest had him beaten and put in the stocks. Jeremiah's first response was to resolve never to speak God's Word again, but he could not: "Then I said, 'I will not make mention of Him, nor speak anymore in His name.' But His Word was in my heart like a burning fire shut up in my bones; I was weary of holding it back, and I could not" (Jer. 20:9 NKJV).

Jeremiah's persistence in telling the truth kept him in trouble with those in power. Jeremiah's story demonstrates that we should not expect a favorable response when we stand against evil. We should expect a fight when we threaten the grip that sin has on people's hearts and minds. But someone reached out to us in spite of the struggle, and so must we.

More than just being a persistent voice, Jeremiah was a lonely voice. Jeremiah spoke these heavy messages to the most powerful people in Judah by himself (Jer. 25). Even when it appears that we might be the only ones standing against evil, we are not excused from taking those stands. It may look as though no one else is standing with us, but we still owe our obedience to the Holy Spirit. Jeremiah understood what it meant to follow God when no one else would; do we?

Not only did Jeremiah speak God's Word persistently and alone, but he also spoke in opposition to the powers of his day. The false prophet Hananiah strongly opposed Jeremiah's lone voice (Jer. 28). It must have been frustrating for Jeremiah to stand and speak as a prophet, only to have another "prophet" stand and directly contradict the Word that the Lord had given him to speak. In the eyes of the people, it was now one prophet's word against another, and Hananiah had public opinion in his favor.

We face a similar situation because we are called to speak the truth in a world full of voices. The waters have been so muddied that it is difficult to even be heard, much less be identified as the truth from among all of the noise, philosophies, religions, and even false voices from within many churches.

At a moment in the story when it becomes difficult to control our blood pressure, Jeremiah reminds us that each prophet should be judged by his words (Jer. 28:8–9). Yes! The man of God stands on the Word of God once again, and so can we. We desperately need to understand that the Word of the Lord is the only sure footing from which to speak against evil and stand against its advances. What Jeremiah demonstrated in this instance was an understanding that our vindication comes from God.

The man who entrusts himself to the Lord's vindication can stand against evil, unfettered by the fearful deception that he will harm his family by his unyielding adherence to the truth. In fact, Matthew 5:11 teaches us that we are "blessed" when we are persecuted and when people say "all kinds of evil" against us "falsely . . . because of [Jesus]" (NASB). If we will accept and even embrace the ire of the depraved, we can be far more effective than we would be if we try to appease the dying world that lashes out at those who tell the truth.

The story gets even better in chapter 36, when King Jehoiakim cut up the scroll containing Jeremiah's message and threw it into the fire. Throughout history, many have tried to destroy the Word of God, either by physical obliteration or by debunking or discrediting its claims. All have failed.[13]

You may be reading Jeremiah's story and wondering to yourself, "What good did his obedience and persistence do? No one even listened to him." But, that's not quite true. The prophet Daniel relays a very important part of Jeremiah's story. This prophet of the Lord, who persisted in his faith in the Word of God in a foreign land, was doing some reading. He wrote, "I, Daniel, understood by the books the number of the years specified by the word of the Lord through Jeremiah the prophet, [Yes!] that he would accomplish seventy years in the desolations of Jerusalem" (Dan. 9:2 NKJV).

Because of Jeremiah's faithfulness, Daniel understood that the time had come for God to restore the Jews from their desolation. Daniel records his response, saying "Then I set my face toward the Lord God to make request by prayer and supplications, with fasting, sackcloth, and ashes" (Dan. 9:3 NKJV). Because of Jeremiah's faithfulness, Daniel knew that he should begin to pray confessing the sins of his people and pleading for their restoration as a people faithful to the Lord.

We may not see the fruits of our obedience to God, and that may cause us to grieve as Jeremiah did. But, we should never lose heart, thinking that our obedience to the Lord is meaningless and that our suffering is wasted. Jeremiah was wildly unpopular and had no following in his day, but God's Word through him awakened hope in one faithful servant of the Lord and led to the restoration of the Jewish people from exile.

We can expect resistance and times when it seems as though no one is listening. We'll be in good company. Pick up the sword that was carried by Jeremiah, Daniel, and so many others whose hearts are eternally bound to ours through the blood of Jesus, and fight the same fight against evil, knowing that the Word that we carry, "is the power of God for salvation to everyone who believes" (Rom. 1:16 NASB).

Make it Count

None of this means anything unless, as Ecclesiastes 12:13 puts it, we "fear God and keep His commandments, for this is man's all" (NKJV). And, First John 3:23-24 clarifies what his commandment is: "This is His commandment, that we believe in the name of His Son Jesus Christ, and love one another, just as He commanded us. The one who keeps His commandments abides in Him, and He in him" (NASB).

Do you trust the one God? Have you put your faith in his Son? God wants every one of us to repent of our sin and to trust him, no matter how far gone we may be. The God who created you wants to secure you safely to himself. The Lord makes it clear that he takes "no pleasure in the death of the wicked, but that the wicked turn from his way and live" (Ezek. 33:11 NASB). We have to understand that he provided one way to be reconciled to him for every soul for all time, and that there is no other. Acts 4:12 teaches us that "there is salvation in no one else; for there is no other name under heaven that has been given among men by which we must be saved" (NASB).

There is a "righteousness of God through faith in Jesus Christ for all those who believe" (Rom. 3:22 NASB). He tells us that "all have sinned and fall short of the glory of God, being justified as a gift by His grace through the redemption which is in Christ Jesus" (Rom. 3:23-24 NASB). Once we have acknowledged our sin and our need for redemption for that sin, we must believe that God provided that redemption through Jesus, his Son. Without his death and resurrection, the penalty for our sin falls hopelessly upon us. Romans 6:23 teaches us that "the wages of sin is death, but the free gift of God is eternal life in Christ Jesus our Lord" (NASB).

We stand undeniably guilty of sin and in need of salvation from its penalty. Because of his love for us, the Almighty God worked salvation for us by fulfilling the requirements of the law through the death and resurrection of his Son. He stands ready to save those who confess with their mouths "Jesus is Lord" and entrust themselves in their hearts to his resurrection (Rom. 10:9–10 NASB).

From there, the Lord wants us to walk with him for the rest of our lives and on into eternity, never to be separated again. He wants to grow us into the men that we want to be, men who fill the roles that our families so desperately need us to fill (Rom. 6:1–14; 8:1–11).

As men of God (or mighty men, as they are called in Second Samuel and around my house), let us stand with both feet on the Word of the Lord. In defiance of every deception, walk on water. In love, let us take up the full armor provided to us by the Almighty God himself. Let us fortify our homes according to the boundaries set by the Lord, and let us teach them diligently to our children. Let us train our children in the use of the ancestral sword by which our forefathers took their stands and have defeated the lie since the beginning.

We have been called and equipped to be nothing less than heroes. I get to be the only man in the history of the world that my children will call "daddy," and I accept! I get to be "the man" to the greatest woman I have ever known and to know her and be known by her like no one else, ever. I get to experientially know what life really is: "that they may know You, the only true God, and Jesus Christ whom You have sent" (John 17:3 NASB).

Through the apostle Paul, the Lord has likened the lives of his followers to a race. To expand upon his comparison, our individual races are like the legs of a relay. History, once complete, will be the story of the triumph of the love of God over evil, out of which he rescues his people, through history's one and only focal figure, Jesus. In that story, his people carry the Word and the work of the Lord. The baton has been carried by a great cloud of witnesses: Enoch, Noah, Abraham, Moses, Joshua, Caleb, Ruth, David, Elijah, Elisha, Daniel, John the Baptist, Joseph and Mary, Peter, Paul, and many more. Some of them have names that we know, most of them have been forgotten by human memory, but all are remembered by the Almighty God. They were fence posts. Now, the baton (the preserved Word of God himself) that they carried has been handed off to us. And, the Lord will sustain us, as he sustained them.

While the nations rage against the Lord and against his Anointed, let us stand in sharp and undeniable contrast to the landscape of hopelessness that dominates the lives of so many souls oppressed by sin's deceit. Let us run with endurance the race that is set before us.

Thank you for reading, and I pray that this message will lead you to seek the one God, and to be ever closer to him. Neither this nor any other book should ever hold a place that even approaches that of the Bible. My intention is, and always will be, to point the way to him, just as other faithful saints have done for me. In the authority of the Almighty God, in the precious and holy name of Jesus, and in the power and guidance of the Holy Spirit, "Remember the Lord, great and awesome, and fight for your brethren, your sons, your daughters, your wives, and your houses" (Neh. 4:14 NKJV).

Endnotes

1. What does it mean to "find yourself?" How about you put down the smartphone, pull out the ear buds, and live for about fifteen minutes. Now see if you don't find yourself in a hurry. "But what if I don't like myself," you ask. Good, that's a perfect place to start. You're showing progress already.

2. Let's stop and savor the flavor of Genesis 6:8, which says: "But Noah found grace in the eyes of the Lord" (NKJV). Noah made a decision to find grace in God's eyes when the rest of the world sought grace in the eyes of man and self. In whose eyes do we find grace? As the men in our homes, relationships, school and work, we will not be able to function correctly and bear up under our responsibilities unless we find grace in our Father's eyes.

3. I put "hear" in quotation marks because I have never audibly heard the voice of the Spirit of the Lord. He can talk to us if he chooses to, but I don't want to have you thinking that one of us is crazy because you don't hear him. The best way that I know to tell you how he works is this: however he chooses to go about it, he just lets you know.

4. William L. Shirer, *The Rise and Fall of the Third Reich: A History of Nazi Germany* (New York: Simon and Schuster, 1960), 249.

5. Michael Schneider, "Exclusive: Disney Channel Breaks New Ground with Good Luck Charlie Episode," *TV Guide*, June 20, 2013, http://www.tvguide.com/news/disney-channel-same-sex-couple-1066972.

6. Miley Cyrus, Twitter post, June 23, 2013, 11:52 a.m., http://twitter.com/mileycyrus.

7. "About Modern Family," *ABC*, accessed May 3, 2016, http://abc.go.com/shows/modern-family/about-the-show.

8. "About Modern Family," *ABC*.

9. "The New Normal," *NBC*, accessed May 3, 2016, http://www.nbc.com/the-new-normal?nbc=1.

10. "The New Normal," *NBC*.

11. Allen B. West, "Choose Your Hero to Confront Jihad," *Allen West Republic* (blog), May 3, 2016, http://allenwestrepublic.com/2013/05/03/allenwest-weekly-wrap-up-via-next_gentv-5313-choose-your-hero-to-confront-jihad/.

12. Ronald Reagan, "A Time for Choosing," *Regan Library*, October 27, 1964, https://reaganlibrary.archives.gov/archives/reference/timechoosing.html.

13. Some archaeologists have set out to disprove biblical claims and have instead discovered evidence that supported those claims. Philosophers have devoted themselves to outsmart God and discredit his Word, and not only have they failed, but many of them even came to trust the Lord along the way.

www.ingramcontent.com/pod-product-compliance
Lightning Source LLC
LaVergne TN
LVHW041547070426
835507LV00011B/972